Becoming a Modest Society

ON DISTINGUISHING OURSELVES

by G.V. Loewen

Strategic Book Publishing
New York, NewYork

Copyright © 2009
All rights reserved – G.V. Loewen

No part of this book may be reproduced or transmitted in any form or by any means, graphic, electronic, or mechanical, including photocopying, recording, taping, or by any information storage retrieval system, without the permission, in writing, from the publisher.

Strategic Book Publishing
An imprint of AEG Publishing Group
845 Third Avenue, 6th Floor - 6016
New York, NY 10022
www.StrategicBookPublishing.com

ISBN: 978-1-60860-633-7

Printed in the United States of America

Book Design: Rolando F. Santos

Contents

Introduction: Rational and Rationalization	1
Moral and Ethical	33
Prudence and Prudishness	65
Bravery and Bravado	89
Criticism and Critique	131
Pessimism and Skepticism	169
Modesty and Humility	203
Epilogue: The Post-Nuclear Age	235
Cited and Suggested Reading	241

*For Jennifer Heller:
a modest society*

The question of who we are does not demand any ultimate answer. What it does require of us is that we respond regularly to it in both the day to day and in our dreams.

Introduction: Rational and Rationalization

MANY OF us believe that we live in the greatest society history has yet witnessed. It may not be the best society of which we are capable, we might accede, but we find it difficult to imagine how other societies could be more impressive than our own. This belief is not mere conceit. Glancing quickly over the course of the history of cultures and civilizations, it appears that *their* achievements leave a different kind of impression upon us than do our own. Yes, we say, we stand on the shoulders of these others, and yes, our ancestors accomplished many amazing things. Yet, because of this, and sometimes in spite of what we may regard as their imagined abilities on other matters, it is we who presently populate the earth and who therefore believe that we stand tallest with regard to the truly enlightened society.

    I can look at every other society of which I have any knowledge at all and say with some confidence that I would rather live now, at this time, and not at any other. I can point to the technical achievements of our society, such as medical advances and feats of engineering. I can nod with some satisfaction at the broadening of enlightened human rights and the fact that we are now more aware of how human differences divide us and make us strange to one another. I can gaze with anticipation and optimism at the horizon of the stars, to which one version of the destiny of humankind beckons us. These social facts of our time appear not only qualitatively different from those outlooks and abilities of any other time; they also appear to us to be *better*.

That we cannot look upon ourselves from any other vantage point in history is taken as a given. With that alone, we might be at least a little suspicious that we could be missing something, that the face in the mirror is at once quite familiar and incomplete, with some details and margins a little fuzzy, and with the larger background, the context within which our personal actions take place, quite shadowy and indistinct. Most of the time this troubles neither our consciousness nor our consciences. Now and then, however, we are made more aware that how we see ourselves is not how others see us, at the individual level or at the cultural level. If this kind of often sudden doubt persists, it may also grow into that larger suspicion that we are not everything we claim to be.

We are familiar with overstating our case in our own biographies. It would be a rare person indeed who could reminisce about all they have done in their lives without wincing or even shuddering. Guilt and bad conscience—the one predicated from moral codes and the other quite personal, contextual, and finding a home in ethics—are a good part of the lot of the vast majority of us, we imagine, and it is this imagining that presents the turning back from introspection that grounds us once again in the larger picture of our culture. Who has not thought this way? This very question allows us to salve our own self-doubt and to regain some sense of composure in the face of lingering questions about our abilities, knowledge, and ideas of right and wrong. We may not be perfect, we say, but who amongst human beings is so? And who amongst us is never human enough to err? It is okay to be human in this world of humanity. It is quite fine with others if we are so. And if we continue to make mistakes we think we ought not to suffer ourselves too precisely. Perhaps it is indeed up to others than ourselves to correct the past, although we are usually willing to play our small part in this endeavor. A single person cannot carry the weight of the world on his shoulders, even though we might sometimes walk the earth as if this was the case. The world's weights are not our personal concern, and cannot be so, given that whatever dubious acts we commit and thoughts we think—dangerous, unconcerned, self-absorbed, or childish—are there to be absorbed into the whole. This is, in fact, the main function our society performs for us. Its solidarity in part means that we are social only in its midst, and the range of sociality allowable by this or that culture, in this or that time or space, takes place because the whole can withstand it, or that such action is functional for its very existence. In this way too, our imagination of what society does for us as human individuals allows all sudden introspection to become at once premature. The old saying *there are things you should not know* is for us altered by our modern outlook, which reacts negatively to any source of authority that attempts to try to tell us what to do. We are more comfortable with the idea that *there are things you do not need to know (or care) about.*

Why this is so is not only due to the bewildering array of human knowledge of our day, of which we are aware in a certain odd way. We *do* know that there are a monstrous lot of things one *could* know about. At the same time, we are more aware that we do not need to know very much of anything about this vastness to get on with our day-to-day lives. We live very much on this basis, and this is the first principle of a kind of rationality that conceives of the great society as efficient and predictable. *Rationalization* is the name for a set of social processes that further the efficiency of the ability to say to ourselves either, *I need to know* or *I do not need to know*, and we apply this rubric to every situation we come across, whether at the trivial level of gossip or at the height of self-destruction and apocalypse. We can protest, if someone might accuse us of willing ignorance or unconcern that it is not possible for each of us to know what might need to be known to live (even) better than we already do. This might be the best we can do, if not as a society at least as individuals. Once again, the very function of the wider society, starting with our intimate companions and friends and family, is to somehow "make up" for our deficits. The reason others are even present, aside from satisfaction of the more immediate desires of the human appetite, is to make good on the timeless sense that the social contract is present precisely to pick up the slack of each of its constituents. Indeed, we do not need to know this or that because we are assured that someone else *does* need to know it and that that other's need is not created by our own inability or ignorance. This is just how society works, and there is an end to it. Further, we can argue that we ourselves pick up the slack for others all the time, whether intimately or amongst nations. We quite rightly might say, at least to ourselves, *I have got my fair share of burdens, don't put any more expectation and obligation on me!* All of this—that there is too much to know about, that we know what we need to know to get by and help others to do the same, and that we should not be expected to pull more weight than the next person—are exceptionally strong in their influence over our beings, as it were. The thought of living otherwise—especially without any immediate evidence that such a life-change would accomplish anything other than further burden us and make us stray from the task of happiness for one and all—is enough to extinguish any effort to try and do so.

This is perhaps the most powerful suasion that allows the *need to know* to migrate to the *want to know,* and similarly its corresponding opposites of the *not need* and the *not want*. To say that *I do not want to know about this* appears at first to be quite different from the idea of need, although we often use the terms interchangeably. The idea of *want* as a form of desire seems to be self-absorbed at worst, self-concerned at best. We can write off *need* as appearing to be more objective, as if everyone else might agree with us that for us to know or do this would be unnecessary in some general sense. The *want*, however, conjures images of selfishness, greed, or even resentment and envy. Yet our idea of need in contemporary Western society is almost indistinguishable from that of want. If we are stricken with the sudden desire to risk ourselves in some manner, great or small, we are equally likely to be told, *no, you do not want to do that* as that we *do not need* to. Far from being the ethical terms they once were, and far from them being able to maintain the distinction between self-centered desire and the desire to advance the common good, want and need have become similar to what the linguistic philosopher Ludwig Wittgenstein called "odd job words." This kind of word is a jack of all trades, appearing here and there as a vehicle for vagaries in our speech and writing. (Later on, we will encounter other terms such as *family* and *religion* that have this itinerant function in language that in fact have no need to be more precise and serve us better as the largest umbrellas.) I'm not saying that we ought to stop using such words but that we might become more honest about our beliefs if we examine their use more closely.

One plausible origin of the older distinction between want and need places their use in the context of a kind of society rather different from our own. If *need* is reserved for denoting an action or thought that places the community above the individual, ultimately there are no individual needs. Indeed, the use of the term *want* might denote a will or action contrary to community fulfillment, and we still have a residue of this way of thinking in certain contemporary contexts, as when we are required to work as a team in the office or on the field. The sociologist Emile Durkheim called this kind of society "mechanical," in reference to the form of solidarity it took on. These small-scale pre-agricultural societies contained like members, not merely in everyone sharing the same "how-to" knowledge about getting on in the day-to-day world but, more profoundly, the same values and beliefs. Each member of the community was socialized in the same manner, and members of the community—not merely the biological parents—functioned as the mentors. Life cycles were short, and expectations of a child's maturity were accelerated to a pace that we today would find onerous or at least astonishing.

Durkheim compared these cultures with those of his day, not qualitatively different from our time, a century later, and found ourselves to be more akin to a biological organism, with a variety of functions and roles. In "organic solidarity" then, members did not in fact know much about each others' roles in society. More telling, and very obvious in our situation in almost any nation-state, persons manifestly did *not* share the same values and beliefs. Hence the origin of law with agrarianism and, with the invention of writing, a recorded legal code that dictated what could be both moral and immoral. We are quite familiar with this kind of society, the direct ancestor to our own, but we remain rather astonished that humans could live, and have lived, very differently from this. We recognize that there are some sectarian communities—the Amish and Hutterites in North America, for instance—who attempt with courage (and perhaps paranoia) to maintain a kind of mechanical solidarity to preserve their culture and their values. Yet it is rare to walk into a Wal-Mart where I live without seeing a few Hutterites shopping there, so there is a sense that even the most conserving of cultures has a difficult row to hoe in the face of the dominant social norms and forms.

Durkheim was by no means nostalgic about the dwindling resonance of mechanical societies but simply wished to point to the fact that human beings are not by nature enthralled to any particular kind of cultural system. Nor did he suggest the romantic possibility of returning to a time when all human beings lived in this manner, as did Rousseau before him, and as Marx and Engels felt could be "modernized" to suit the needs of our own time in "communism." There was, in fact, no true *need* to do either, for Durkheim, but to improve the functioning of organicity in a way that it satisfied more and more of the needs of individuals as they were. In other words, we did not need to change in any fundamental manner to create the great society. In fact, when we witness the amazing variety of such systems, including those of kinship, religion, and education, to name a few, we are often pushed back into the very center of the *do not need to know* circle. By implication, those of us living "organically," because we cannot perform the roles of others, and because we do not necessarily share any of their beliefs and values, cannot take their places if they perish.

Perhaps the easiest way to think about this distinction in human social forms is to realize that in small-scale communalistic cultures, the whole equals the sum of its parts, in that each member portrays the same "amount" of culture to another member. If one dies—which we imagine was often the case in cultures born of nature but now irrevocably set apart from it by language, tools, bipedalism, and brain size—another can replace them immediately. Not so in culture of today. One has to negotiate specific training of replacement elements, for in organic society the whole is *greater* than the sum of its parts. Durkheim did not mean to say that our society was better than its proposed primordial version but that how it functioned was qualitatively distinct, and that this change comes about in full force with the invention of perennial and sedentary agriculture, some ten thousand years ago.

What does all of this have to do with *needs* and *wants*? We have already suggested that in communal societies there are no individual needs, quite simply because the concept of the one and the many are united in a manner we find strange today. We are used to being able to partially identify with other people; we might say that we empathize with them or we "feel their pain" or joy. Yet in a society of hundreds of millions, let alone the emerging global society, such a thought becomes immediately rhetorical and abstract. We might imagine placing ourselves in the shoes of others, but clearly the diversity of the human situation disallows any long-term identification, and rarely does it suggest to us that we should in fact *change* our values to suit others, or that we *need* to step outside of our culture to approach that of the other. Rather, it appears that only in death are we united (this somewhat disconcerting idea will reappear much later in this book when we come face to face with our own version of the apocalypse).

If there are no needs other than that of the community and if all agree that this must be so, the idea of *want* slips away in the same manner as does that of the individual. Yet this kind of thinking appears to be in stark contrast to our own. Yes, we have proceeded to make the distinction between the need and the want, the many and the one, but of late we have seen them become virtually indistinguishable once again. Ironically, this may be a similar situation to what the first humans found themselves in, with the glaring difference that we have inverted the order of value of the terms in question. More often than not, today it is the individual, rather than the community, that has "needs-wants." How did this occur, and is there any real problem with such a shift in values?

The idea that the community benefits by the efforts and desires of individuals within it is a very recent one. Along with this, we also imagine that persons are somehow more real than communities. Society is a reification, an abstract concept made into a thing. We cannot point to a *society* in the same way we can observe a person. With the advent of modern science, we have taken to a bias toward the physically real and a bias against what some have called "metaphysics." With the collapse of wants and needs into one another interpreted as pragmatic, one might also understand the loss of interest in the abstract as directed by a certain utility.

What practical purpose could the great bulk of philosophy serve? Science at least gives us things we desire as well as things we—at least in massive organic society— actually need to have, or, at the very least, things that work to further our new interests. It is a little premature and casual to define the distinction between the physical (what we feel the world and ourselves are made of) and the metaphysical (speculative meanderings of the mind's eye and its ideals) as solely the same distinction between science and philosophy. Rather, science, too, has its own abstractions—who has *seen* gravity, for instance, or magnetism?—and philosophy itself has many schools of thought If the latter seems vague and undefined, we can look to the simple response of the modern German philosopher Hans-Georg Gadamer when he reminds us that "life is vague," and that thinking—at base, what philosophy is about, presumably—is about, first and foremost, life itself. We might go a little farther than this, and in fact my favorite "definition" of philosophy runs something like this: "Philosophy is not a body of knowledge, it is the vigilance that reminds us of the source of all knowledge." This comes from the French existential philosopher Maurice Merleau-Ponty. As with much such writing, it first appears rather unhelpful, more about what

Introduction: Rational and Rationalization

it is not than what it is, another classic complaint of the pure pragmatist. Yet the source of all knowledge is obviously a combination of human experience and human reflection, or thinking about one's experience. For philosophy to be a more disciplined version of these universal abilities of all of humankind reminds us of not only the source of the fruits of thinking—knowledge and its manifestations—but also of the source of that very humanity. Now we have, all of a sudden, a better sense concerning why there may be a problem with the inability to distinguish between words and concepts, on the one hand, and when and where singular terms can do us a world of good, on the other.

The human process of experience and reflection—the basis for philosophy, amongst other things—holds within it this double tendency. That is, our experience of the world can either reaffirm previous prejudices, or shatter them. Our thinking about our lives can both rationalize them and allow us to repeat our actions and routines, or to question them rationally and perhaps alter them. It is no doubt often more convenient to live on in the former manner, without critical reflection and instead using one's experiences as reaffirmations and rationalizations. For our society and its members, it appears that only crises of various kinds, personal and social, might push us to the latter manner of living—that of serious reflection and the changing of previous prejudice. Hence the movement to what could be cast as unconcern might have yet another logistical decision at its base: We have created a society in which the vast majority of us have no need to question our experiences within it.

As the American sociologist Peter Berger suggests, borrowing a famous phrase from Jean Paul Sartre, society can be a massive occasion for the wallowing in "bad faith" inasmuch as we might come to believe we have no choice about actions in our lives. Theoretically, society can equally be a source of human freedom, but from the existential standpoint, it appears very few of us regularly use society in this manner, preferring to run along its tracks with little deviation. Of course, it is one thing to accuse ourselves of bad faith when the consequences for deviance—including that of thinking—are sometimes fatal. Loss of jobs, spouses, friends and family, even our general sociality as we have known it, are threats that warn off potential transgressors of social norms. Yet Berger is quick to remind us that all of these things ultimately will pass anyway, that we are, in Sartre's phrase, "condemned to freedom," with our deaths merely being the final reminder of this. We avoid this rather agonizing understanding of human existence by constructing a prison-like society around us and then quite cooperatively living in it and volunteering to maintain it and our captivity.

All of this seems rather grandiose. Do we really feel all that existential angst at the thought of the ultimate nakedness of human life and its relatively short-term qualities? What of all of the satisfactions, loves, fulfillments, responsibilities that the day to day presents to us as cooperative citizens and responsible adults? Surely not all of these are hollow, even though we are aware of their transience and that we must apparently face death alone. Is this not the whole problem with philosophizing, in that it takes what are essentially mundane circumstances and vaults them onto metaphysical pedestals? Perhaps there is another way to get there from here. Our very idea of what is essential to us is enshrined in philosophical ideals, and the distinction between what is merely mundane and what is essential is born in the realm of those ideals. Once again, we may have fallen into the trap of forcing terms to conform to one another and thus identifying with their alters. Like wants and needs becoming one, the essential and the mundane can now be described as having like use. What is of the day to day is of essence, not extraordinary feelings or abnormative events. Once again, the triumph of a certain kind of use of modern science suggests to us that there are no other essences than those of the day-to-day world, which are in their turn observable and measurable and *usable*. *Mundane* need no longer appear as a pejorative, in the same way that *want* should not arouse our suspicions that someone is being selfish. We in fact live in the world as it is, and not some realm transcendent to this world. This other realm, if it even exists, can at the very least wait for us to pass along to it. In the meanwhile, we have a job to do, a life to live, and convenient rails to run on in doing so.

However more efficient it may be to charge the mundane realm with the characteristics reserved in previous epochs for the essential, it does give us a clue to the uneasy relationship the two have had historically. If we are now fusing them, refusing to acknowledge time-honored philosophical and religious differences that were said to exist between them, we might legitimately question whether such relations were ever so different as the scions of these two forms of human thought and belief claimed. Ideas of philosophical and religious weight have always come from the elites of society—as long as society functioned in an organic manner that in turn produced these elites—and only after their formulation did some of them find a home in the hearths of regular people.

The great social scientist Max Weber suggests that this is indeed how new religious movements get started. Not so much that elite sectors of society—in Weber's theory, recently displaced intellectual classes who had been marginalized from the centers of political power by warrior castes or economic forces—provided the actual persons, prophets, or messiahs for new religions or philosophies, but that their ideas were taken up by already marginal class persons who became their mouthpieces and vehicles.

Within this new franchise they are said to take on their "magical" content, re-enchanting the margins of the social world that were never near power, ironically unlike the originators of the ideas. Perhaps even more ironic is that the intellectuals who originally invented the ideas never seriously believed in them, at least as agents of social, let alone spiritual, transformation. If the career of these new ideas was successful in changing things, ultimately they become part of the new ruling relations of a set of social institutions, which, with final irony, looked remarkably like the ones they displaced.

The careers of Christianity after Augustine and the ideals of the French, American, and socialist revolutions are excellent examples of this process of rationalization, which Weber called *routinization.* In this word one can recognize the very kernel of our convenient and efficient collapsing of what used to be very different words into one another, the word "routine." We may well be warned to "expect the unexpected," but we know in our contemporary society that the unexpected is rare and, furthermore, usually undesirable. We are very aware that we could not function smoothly in a world fraught with inconsistency and inaccuracy, and we often become annoyed when it raises its fuzzy head before us. Yet we are also, perhaps dimly, aware that the great majority of humanity in our own time live in precisely this manner, partly due to the way in which we in fact do live. This tension, which can never be entirely collapsed, is likely at the heart of our recent ability to fuse once unlike concepts as *want* and *need* or *mundane* and *essence.*

If thinkers such as Weber are correct, all revolutionaries within society, and the revolutionary longings within us, must be sobered. For no matter the charismatic quality of the original ideas or their bearers, even if assigned by God or the gods, the wider society they sought to change gradually gets the better of them, and such changes that at first appeared radical to what had gone before are assimilated by rationalization. Change does occur, and Weber distinctly thought that *charisma*, a word that appears in the Greek New Testament and that he uses for an altered purpose in describing the character or presence of a prophetic leader, was in fact a major agent of the dynamic of history. But such change as there may be is in fact not at all as revolutionary as the new movement's followers might have imagined or desired.

It is evidently the same for us as individual persons, whether or not we attach ourselves to larger groups that ostensibly share, or publicly claim to share, beliefs new or old. New Year's resolutions are a case in point. Let us say you wish to get in shape, and purchase exercise equipment to do so, in the comfort of your own home. Perhaps whimsically, social science has collected data on just how many people follow through with this particular desire, and many others, for that matter. The short answer to this is, simply, not many. On radio and television talk shows, as well as in therapists' offices, much of the conversations and plaintiffs that take place concern our inability to follow through with sundry and diverse life changes of varying profundity. We are, in this very real sense, microcosms of human history, just as we often remain enthralled to the inertia of our own biographies. Is it reasonable for us to criticize ourselves for being apparently unable to stand up against the forces of inertia that seem to betray what we want to be to that which we have been? In other words, who we wish to become must come out of who we do not wish to remain.

Just as with great historical movements of ideas, religions, politics, and what have you, the more modest changes we attempt in our own personal lives must come face to face with how we have lived. In doing so, we become painfully aware of not only the convenience and efficiency of our routines and habits, but that all of those around us conspire to keep us on those tracks and perhaps question in various ways any kind of change in us. For change in one person requires a change in others around them. If I wish to become someone else, even in some small way, others must adjust to this change. Is it reasonable to expect others to do so, in the name of progress, evolution, freedom, enlightenment, or some other goal, the means to which may be halting and sporadic?

This potential dilemma suggests yet another possible collapsing of two unlike concepts into a yet more unlikely unison. This time, however, we are not content with merely thinking about characteristics of the human condition as invariant and in identity. In contemplating personal or cultural change, we might well expect the other to absorb, forgive, or change with us, whether that other is writ large or small. But surely an even more convenient attitude to adopt would be to see the other as another self, who or which would also adapt or adopt the changes we are interested in if either only they could do so, or could do so but were not so apparently pigheaded or backward. Perhaps they merely need a role model, which further rationalizes the change that we are hoping to make for ourselves. Why not be the leader, we might say, and why not pave the way for others to make correspondingly impressive and even necessary changes in their own lives or in their social organizations? This kind of thinking, born on the same template as the collapse of wants and needs and the mundane and the essential, allows a package of comfortable self-affirmations to be delivered to us. Not only can we accomplish the change we desire, or at least attempt it, without concern or bad conscience regarding imposing a corresponding change in others, but in fact we can demonstrate to these others that such changes as we are making are good for all involved, and that the rest of "us," or those others whom we label as "them," would do best to follow our lead in all matters.

Introduction: Rational and Rationalization

No doubt, our modern attitude to non-Western cultures, as well as to the margins of our own culture, whether these are political, economic, religious, or scientific, is based in part on this convenient collapse of categories. In order for us to choose the best route according to our desires, the foundational element of choice must adhere to any possible social situation. Indeed, this is one of our common, if casual and unreflective, definitions of freedom. More than this, *freedom* is a concept that might well animate all human beings, even though we are dimly aware that most other cultures never developed the version of freedom our enlightenment West espouses and, like as not, avoids in the manner Sartre described. Yet the idea of freedom, the nebulous feeling of "being free" is such a good in itself for us that we find it difficult to imagine a life without at least its promise. Those who work all the healthiest and most vital parts of their lives in jobs they do not love, those who co-exist in families or communities that do not represent their ideals, and those who live on the margins of our market economy, unable to consume and participate yet forced to endure the endless advertisement of the "good life" everywhere they look, might well imagine that freedom, from these contexts and from many others, is the Pandoran hope that ironically banishes these other evils, if only it would come.

A society is both an occasion for human freedom and a convenient manner of escaping it. In the more existential version of the concept, choice can present an agony very unlike the feeling when we must choose between competing brands or commodities. I recently purchased a new vehicle, and it took me about six months to choose one. During that time I felt pushed and pulled amongst the competing claims, and all the more so amongst the competing experiences of test driving the actual objects in question. In the end, however theatrically one might appear to emote regarding the gift of one car in the face of the sacrifice of another, *agony* is not the term to use. Rather, the agony of choice appears to us when we face the more profound consequences of having to change our lives in the face of society at large. As always, the philosophical ideal is a little too simple for the reality of the work at hand. Feeling un-free? Well, get a new life. More likely than this, given the consequences of fundamental change in either our own biographies or institutions or even whole societies, the version we encounter in the day to day would run: "Feeling trapped? Then *escape*." In doing so, we turn again to participating in the mundane choices of the market, as I did when confronted with the desire for a new car.

Yet we can pause here again. We already had collapsed what was essential into the mundane, so how can we feel contempt or pangs of conscience regarding such action? Is not such action after all, all in all? Are not my wants twinned with my needs? Are not others desiring the same things as myself, and wish they could do as I did, and yet further might well do so after observing my gallant acts of both choice and change?

It is clear that making a choice that takes us either toward or away from rationalized means does not necessarily entail rational motives. Aside from the fundamental lack of rationality in believing that others must be or even desire to be the same as ourselves, there is as well the sense that efficiency and convenience, measurability and predictability have at their disposal all possible rational motivations. The belief that this is so is also, ironically, not rational. This tandem of misplaced beliefs in the rational follows us whether or not we disdain the modern world and seek to create another one, or we embrace the world as it is and shun what other worlds there may in fact also be. This is so because we either assume that what has been rationalized is inherently subject to irrationality and thus what it means to be rational is to turn away from the world, or we assume that the modern rationalized world is so precisely due to its inherent rationality, and thus to follow along in all things contemporary is to also be, by definition, part of the rationality. As with need and want, *essential* and *mundane*, and *self* and *other*, *rational* and *rationalized* are, in this latter view, collapsed.

As we have already observed, therein lays an ethical flaw, as well as one of logic. Rationalization proceeds apace due to a myriad of motives associated not with a specific, reflective and critical school of enlightenment philosophy called *rationalism*, but instead with bureaucratic structures and institutions that are the hallmark of capitalism. What can be most efficient, what is the one "best" way of doing things, and what provides the best cost-operations option, are indeed reflected upon, but only in the most narrow sense of the term. To rationalize a process is yet also different from finding an excuse for something we have done personally or politically, often casually called rationalizing, as in "you are just rationalizing this away." The confusions, which at this point are becoming more strident, are not merely semantic. Rationalism spawns rational thought; a specifically reflective and idealistic form of philosophical critique, holistic and encompassing of scientific method and the methods of doubt first enshrined boldly in Descartes, but available in most other thinkers since his time. Rationality is another term that is an offspring of this set of conceptions. Rationalization is something to which a ratio—a quantitative calculation sometimes rendered as percentages, such as those involved in evaluating "cost-effectiveness," for example—has been applied. It often means that a process, a social context or interaction, has been judged mathematically, either in terms of time, energy, output of product, or economic cost. The result of this kind of judgment, which is, admittedly a kind of reflection but as one can see, with a narrow set of rubrics that are neither critical nor reflective in the broader philosophical sense of the root concept, is that whatever process in question becomes *rationalized*, with the ostensible sense that something has been improved, almost always something material.

Now confusing rational and rationalization does not seem at first to be as convenient for our accustomed habits of thinking as do the three other tandems we have already broached. What would be the point of collapsing a philosophical school inside a logistical or instrumental analysis of material relations? Just so, aside from the prestige or potentially undeserved status the logic of production might accrue if one could claim that it was based in a major pinion of modern thought, one might wish to argue that if we as moderns claim that what is rational is the *best* form of thinking, better than that nonrational (e.g., religious), and certainly better than the pathological *irrational*, then what comes forth from the best thought is the best practice. Those "best practices," a phrase often heard in management models and leadership seminars, can appear to be based in the kind of conceptual thinking that freed our minds from superstition, allowed us to sequester our emotions, and let us loose upon the earth and cosmos with the new arsenal of scientific tools and methods. What could be better?

We are all aware of the fruits of science, although the well-known science educator Carl Sagan famously and quite rightfully notes that we tend to accept these fruits and reject scientific methods (more on that later). The modern miracles of medicine and engineering create a better quality of life and greater longevity for many, potentially for all. The shadow of complete annihilation aside, rational thought and its specific technical fruits are all in all for us, and most would not imagine nor care to live without them. Hence we can understand at least the sometimes calculated penchant for confusing rational and rationalization, and indeed, they are not entirely to be divorced historically. Yet we are also aware that rationalization gives rise to contexts that make no sense to us, and are in fact irrational, as the contemporary American sociologist George Ritzer has remarked.

The very word *bureaucracy*, originally a mere description of an institution based on the office model (*bureau* being French for *office*), has essentially become a pejorative, a term of opprobrium, as in "that is so bureaucratic" or "he is nothing but a bureaucrat." The proselytization of rationalized applied science has given rise to anti-science movements both in the nonrational worlds of religious beliefs, as well as in purely secular "humanist" or humanitarian ideas as in some environmental movements. Rationalization, in a nutshell, is not ultimately rational. Philosophical rationalism, though its market may be narrow and elite, never betrays itself by falling into either the nonrational realm of what it regards as the previous metaphysics—that of religious values or folk nonscience beliefs—nor into the irrational. Though the source of the confusion is not like the others we have discussed in that it does not originate in our personal everyday lives and their conflicts, collapsing the two may be convenient for us at a personal level because it reaffirms the other sets of collapsed concepts, allowing us to think that ultimately our society knows the right way of doing things and, therefore, also has an obligation to the unenlightened to share these best practices.

The desire to "spread the good word" of what we ourselves feel good about is likely a latter-day manifestation of one of the fundamental traits of Western religions. Weber suggests that our culture is born from the roots of not merely religions, which have a radical idea of a realm other to this earth and its mortal life—heavens and hells of various kinds, for example—but that the primary goal of the faithful while still in this mortal world is to spread the message of faith to any and all.

We can see direct reflections of this missionizing bent in our penchant for spreading the rather less religious gospels of our politics, economics, weapons systems, and sexualities around the world. Coupled with the error that reaffirms our desire to see the other as ourselves, and to believe that humans rather unlike ourselves would desire to be as we are if only we helped them out, has created much of the global conflict so in evidence in our contemporary scene.

The history of religious proselytization is also largely one of war and bloodshed. Christianity and Islam have spread their word at the point of the sword, most notably in the early Islamic conquest of the southern Mediterranean and Iberia, and about a millennium later, with the Christian conquistadors in the Americas. To note that these world-historical events made a mockery of the ethics of the respective religions is sadly to acknowledge Weber's understanding of the rationalization processes that even the greatest human ideas undergo when faced with the generally less noble desires of human beings living in the world as it is. The rationalization of the best of what the West may have had to offer the world continues apace today. But we must look to our own society for the forces that generate these processes and not project our anxieties and doubts we may have about the way we live on persons hailing from very different cultures and places.

To do so involves us in yet another kind of irony. Although Western religions have this seemingly unique trait of wishing to "spread the word," the collapsing of various pairs of unlike concepts in fact leads communities to turn inward. The inwardness of local knowledge is well known to exhibit so-called *ethnocentrism*, the belief that one's own culture or social group is superior to others—sometimes, all others. Religion is an infamous source of rationalizing this tendency, which in fact predates the kinds of organized religious beliefs with which we are familiar. Ethnographic

Introduction: Rational and Rationalization

studies the world over have consistently found that even small-scale pre-agrarian groups have an intense suspicion, bordering on xenophobia, of their neighbors down the river, or in the next valley. So much for cultural evolution, the cynics might chastise, if we are still following these early models of social organization now writ large with global forces of mass destruction.

There is more than meets the eye, here, however. Low population load and subsistence lifeways lend themselves to a "go with the flow" kind of attitude, and it is anthropologically correct to also observe that in societies that have lived very near what we imagine to be the "state of nature," although still cultural and still human, in fact do not tend to exhibit these xenophobic tendencies. Their style is to set up detailed systems of kin networks and reciprocating access to resource strategies. It was these kinds of societies that Durkheim used as models for his notion of "mechanical solidarity." The vast portion of human tenure on this planet was lived in these forms. As soon as one begins to see strain on resources, higher population loads, and some internal social hierarchy, then we find the beginnings of intergroup competition and conflict that we know so well in its modern form. Once again, there is no point in nostalgically wishing a return to the origins of the social contract, as did Rousseau and as practiced in part by certain Anabaptist sects in North America today. Such a world is forever out of reach and may indeed have been rendered so romantically by students of humanity to be more about our own longings to escape our current dilemmas than about any past reality.

Whatever may be the case here, it is clear that certain forms of social organization have different responses to environmental and internal cultural stress, and that it is not a one-way street from these stressors to intercultural conflict. This is not dissimilar to the well-worn adages of a popular psychology, in that when we have stress we must find some constructive and positive way to cope with it, instead of taking it out on others. Indeed, projecting our internal stress onto others will very likely increase stress in all quarters, especially over the long term. Hence we encounter the second implication of local knowledge and its ability to ironically turn away from the world while at the same time holding the wider world responsible for its apparent ignorance of the "one best way." This is the notion of having a proprietary attitude toward one's own culture or community. Not only is local knowledge tinged with ethnocentrism, it also wishes to possess itself in an odd way. "These are our ways" is a common statement to be heard when visiting a foreign culture. As well, they have been handed down from ancestral tradition. "Our parents and grandparents did it this way, it is simply what we do" or "how we think." We should be mistaken that these apparently benign statements have any hint of relativism imbedded in them. It is true that once in while we may find a native of whatever stripe saying to us that "this is what *we* do, but you have no need of doing it," but this is rare—and for good reason, if we take the native's point of view to shed light on our own proclivities. If some of us in any culture admitted that our ways were simply the local variant of human diversity without inherent superiority and therefore had no *natural* claim on us, then whatever culture we espouse would immediately become fragile and in danger of disappearing. If we admit that we could do otherwise than "what we do," then what we do is exposed as parochial and, at best, geared toward a practical purpose. No higher rationalization for the existence of what we do here would be possible, as our once "best" practices are now seen in the light of all other practices, which themselves have the same claims to either "the best" or "just what we do and you can do what you want, it doesn't matter."

Introduction: Rational and Rationalization

We may think it a little childish of any cultural group, including our own, to have to imagine implausible defenses for its social organizations and practices—whether it be gods, or mythical ancestors who were more than human, or the wisdom of animal spirits, or enlightenment philosophies of utilitarianism, to name a few—but it is not some other group's ideas that must be defended against. Rather, it is the ever-pressing question of *why is this done* that must be extinguished in the human breast. This is so because such questions—asked by children of all cultures and times in their minions—ultimately prove fatal to any society solely bent on reproducing itself. As well, and perhaps ultimately, the *why* questions interrogate cultural practice. These are very different from the other kind of why questions children also ask that seek scientific explanation of nature and the cosmos. These other kinds of questions in fact are *how* questions and not truly *why* questions at all, as in *why is the sky blue?* Such a question elicits a response that speaks of the process of physical forces rather than tell us *why* this is so. Rather, the *why* questions concerning cultural practices ultimately relate to the question of the mortal human condition: Why are we here and why *here*? As no culture has an objectively valid answer to *that* question, rationalization appears the only choice in the face of the void. The proprietary attitude taken by members of a cultural or social in-group becomes understandable not only logistically and existentially but also with a view to that group's own long-term viability in the case of competition from other groups.

Sectarian communalist groups with Anabaptist roots are a common North American example of the deliberate self-imposed relative isolation calculated to preserve this or that culture from assimilation. We are, in the mainstream of North American society, usually quite tolerant, if somewhat disdainful and bemused, with these groups' attempts. We are aware that we might do the same thing in their shoes, even though we do not abandon our self-assured sense of superiority in thinking that in part because we are *not* in their shoes that we *do* know better after all. Obviously, our level of tolerance depends on many factors. Are these subcultures a threat to the wider society, and in what manner? Are they critical and offensive in some other way to the values we cherish? Are they growing at our expense, or do they claim or actually have some material privilege we also claim or that is claimed by all and yet not evenly distributed? With the Amish, old-order Mennonites, and Hutterites, for example, none of these questions has any real force. Rather, these groups present perhaps some of our ideals which, though laced with nostalgia and romanticism, we might wish to ideally pursue. Living in an intimate community with more value solidarity and group concern over the well-being of individuals, less self-interest, less consumptive and energy expensive, concern for elders and with an instrumental use of material goods (rather than a worship of them for their own sake or for the status we can borrow from owning or using them), and, finally, a stolid and stoic work ethic are just some of the ideals apparently espoused and actually lived by these kinds of groups. In a sense, we are tolerant of them because they remind us of some of our own ideals, however shrouded by modern social relations.

However, not all subcultures fair as well in the midst of a dominant society. Other related groups also ostensibly based on reformation religions and their offspring, Doukhabors and certain quasi-Mormon sects, for example, are examined quite critically indeed and are often subject to fines and other legal measures, mainly because they practice polygamy. And in cases where we judge the transgressions of our ideals more extreme, the results might be catastrophic for the subculture, as was the case for the Branch Davidian sect near Waco, Texas. So even if the historical sources of the subcultures align with the sources of the wider society,

Introduction: Rational and Rationalization

there is no guarantee that we will put up with the diversity to which in descending generations any genealogy is prone. The questions of changing standards of what is or what is not to be tolerated by the mainstream, as well as charges of hypocrisy directed against it, are often well founded. Yet ultimately it is not the transgression of the norm that is crucial to our reaction. What allows our reaction is the combination of greater physical and symbolic force and the sense that our ideas are inherently superior to those of the subculture, even if they represent some of our ideals in an "old-fashioned" form. All the more decisive is when the subculture represents ideals in the form of repressed desires, such as power and control, including sexual control, over other human beings in an intimate setting. In these cases, such as the suspected but apparently unfounded suspicions recently directed at a quasi-Mormon commune in Texas, we may well view persons living there as acting out something we might secretly admire and wish for ourselves. This repression of a desire, and thence the punishing of those who do not repress it, probably animates much of our discomfort with the polygynist sects. ('Polygny' is the correct term for multiple females)

It is clear at least that we have the ability to enforce our moral and legal standards on whomever we please, if we accept the consequences, which may include violence and even death. We are, in a very real way, willing to both die and kill for our cause, yet due to the rationalized structure of the apparatus of the nation state, we can act at a distance, as it were. The role-specialization of organic solidarity not only fosters the disintegration of shared values—say, those that may animate the subculture due to its small-scale intimacies—but maintains and abets their diversity and the conflict that stems from it. Professional keepers of order, those whom the American sociologist Howard Becker calls "rule enforcers," are charged with punishing transgressors of all kinds, either deeply within the dominant society or on its margins. It is important to also note that we can even make rules at a distance. The rule makers in mass democracies are certainly not individual, private citizens like us but those who represent us and what are claimed to be our interests, usually in some very indirect manner. The *rationality* behind this should be obvious: How could society function if everyone had an equal say in its functioning? This does, in fact, work in very small-scale societies, where the politics is by consensus and the gaining of consensus takes all the time it needs to take. We have long since abandoned this mode of the *polis* and for the last ten thousand years or so have practiced versions of what we know today in its most *rationalized* form. Once again we encounter, this time in an organizationally fundamental way, the collapsing of the rational and the rationalized. It may indeed be rational to divide the political labor amongst certain professionally trained role players and add to them a sprinkle of populist politicians just to put a neighborly face on the institutional and governmental processes, but in action the mass of large-scale bureaucracies becomes behemoth-like, as Hobbes long ago predicted. The inertia of rule-keeping and the ritual of rule-making are the hallmarks of such institutions, and we are aware that even the most mainstream of our comrades in consumer capital have a healthy distrust of government in almost all its forms. In this sense, we may look again with some longing at the subcultures that have deliberately taken themselves out of the rationalized spaces of the modern state and constructed a latter-day version of mechanical solidarity in their own local politics.

Yet we are missing something crucial if we only compare the extremes of self-evident small-scale subcultures with an assumed preponderance of homogeneity in the so-called dominant society. For within this latter, and clearly ensconced within its relations of production and politics, are many other "regions of sociality," their members more or less conforming to the dominant ideals and more or less exhibiting their norms. No doubt this kind of view can be taken to its logical nth degree, if we, living in a society that prizes the individual and his or her talents, suggest that each one of us is an imperfect version of some ideal citizen or even human being. We are, indeed, members of categories that are real and not abstract. We are, as Weber noted, "historical types" and not "ideal types." In his analysis, the word *ideal* is not to be taken as the *best*, as the same word connotes in our casual speech, but simply as "abstracted from reality." Each of these broad regional categories does not act out in the way true subcultures or sectarians do, by attempting to banish from their lives all but traces of the wider culture. Rather, we and others like us want to participate in the dominant culture, but from our own angles. Some of us may indeed seek to dominate what has become dominant and change it to more of our liking. The so-called neoconservative political movements in North America have attempted to do this since around 1980, with varying success. We should not be surprised by such attempts coming from any quarter that has not abandoned participation, because any system that has the mandate of making and enforcing rules for vast numbers of persons runs the risk of being at odds with all of them, even if in a minor way for many.

Our awareness of these regions of participation is punctuated by unexpected popular crises and what sociologists call "moral panics," whether these be contrived or happenstance. Very often a mixture of both, these passing upheavals call to conscious mind both the unwritten rules of normative and *good* or correct behavior and, also, somewhat more disconcertingly, remind us of what we all are capable of in defense of things that we indeed value even if our cognizance of them is most times mute.

The recent furor surrounding the popular music group The Dixie Chicks and their lead's 2003 comments about then-president G.W. Bush and the ongoing conflicts in the Middle East is an excellent example of both unexpected regional transgression and corresponding reaction thereto. Comments concerning "shame" about sharing the same state of birth as the former President prompted a vitriolic response by many of the group's most avid fans. As well, radio stations in their hundreds refused to play the band's music, often at the request of overwhelming numbers of actual listeners. Although the succeeding years saw the popularity of both that president and the Iraq war plummet, suggesting that the singers' comments were indeed prescient, it is unclear whether the band has reclaimed radio airtime on their traditional country networks. One can also compare record sales of their first three albums, all of which sold well over ten million units, with their most recent offering of 2006. In the latter case, despite garnering all five Grammy awards for which it was nominated, sales as of last year had apparently topped out at about two million. Nothing to complain about, one might suggest, but the relative paucity of sales is perhaps suggestive that the real issues here were neither to do with disloyalty to a nation state nor the well-known conservative tendencies of most country music fans, who tend to be white, rural, and from the lower classes. There is also the biographical fact that two of the three principles in the band do not in fact hail from this typical, perhaps stereotypical, social background. The furor thus strikes the sociologist as odd for these reasons: It lasts beyond the turn in popular opinion nationally, it is directed at a band that does not necessarily represent in its membership the same social groups that generally listen to its music, and the style of the most recent recording is not at all the usual country or even bluegrass for which the band became musically famous and popular in the first place. Perhaps merely the change in musical style can account for the relative lack of sales, but I think there is something deeper at issue here.

Although we will have more to say later on about the heroism of the lonely voice that speaks out against the tide of public or political fashion, I think the betrayal felt by the former fans of this band had little to do with politics per se. Rather, the Dixie Chicks' music and image represented to the dominant society facets of a subaltern regional society within our midst, one that has been seriously disenfranchised by other larger social forces, including those economic and political, cultural, and intellectual. This other society appears, once again, in much of the twenty percent of the overall population of the United States that is in fact designated by the census as rural. These folks are white, from marginal social classes, and exhibit conservative political and moral behaviors.

Though identifying oneself or one's subculture with any aspect of popular culture, no matter how recognizable it may seem, is certainly a risk for any of us; the betrayal of this identification by a musical group no doubt took fans by such surprise that their adoration quickly turned to disdain, even outright hatred in some cases. It is well known, if perhaps irrational, how love can turn to its opposite on a dime of sudden and radical betrayal. In this case, a disenfranchised regional culture is already insecure in its very premise, its very rationale for continuing to exist in the face of dominant and intrusive mainstream ideas and behaviors. The culture from which most country fans are drawn is regularly ridiculed by media and sneered at by the vast majority of North Americans. They are called *racist, ignorant, parochial,* and *redneck,* amongst many other epithets. Yet it is also well-known sociologically that persons who exhibit these kinds of traits, when they have any empirical grounds at all, apparently suffer from a combination of lack of opportunity to access dominant intellectual and cultural resources, are economically marginalized, and also lack the language of social class and politics to air complaints that would be taken more seriously by mainstream institutions. It is reasonable to suggest that in the United States, class conflict is often cloaked in a language of race, not merely due to the historical fact that non-whites tend to be economically marginalized. But in no way does ethnicity or "race" exhaust the relevant variables in any analysis of social hierarchies and their perpetuation. Whatever we may generally imagine this regional culture to be actually like, it is clear that their own imagination includes being more publicly heard through country music, and, specifically included a relatively large audience through the Dixie Chicks, who outsold every other musical entertainment act in the United States from 1998 to 2006. They are also currently the top-selling female group of all time in any genre of popular music, and also the top country group in sales, male or female—all this in a wider culture whose traditions of monotheistic religions make it much easier for persons to identify with a singular popular icon on stage or otherwise. Whether or not this particular band regains its traditional fan base or continues to develop in a new direction remains to be seen. The point that is of greater interest is the ironic action of rationalization in the face of betrayal and threat and in defense of an identity that was thought to be securely represented. Let us use the phrase "nonrational rationalization" to denote this kind of activity. As we have seen, it can be vitriolic and seemingly spontaneous, although it is often co-opted by political interest groups seeing an opportunity to widen their ambit and get *their* message out.

    The case of the Dixie Chicks cannot but call to mind the most famous case of the defense of identity from this same regional culture that levied against The Beatles from 1965 to 1966. John Lennon's notorious remark of the band being "more popular than Jesus" provoked an even greater though

Introduction: Rational and Rationalization

similar reaction from the same cultural region's previous generation. That these kinds of reactions are not rational is due not merely to their emotive quality, which borders on the traits of xenophobia discussed above, but that they are often in error, either beforehand or after the fact, about the identity relation that is ostensibly being protected. In the case of The Beatles, their four members actually were from the homologous class background and social location as their protesters, albeit from another country. As stated, the majority of the Dixie Chicks are not. It is possible that persons identified with The Beatles in fact correctly at first, and then felt betrayed by them due to the unexpected exposure of unshared cultural assumptions, and it is likely that fans identified with the Dixie Chicks more or less incorrectly due to their image and musical styles, and thus were again confounded when the values assumed to be shared were in fact not. A final irony is that the lead singer *is* in fact from the same cultural background and social location as the legions of her disgruntled fans, which only increases the level of discomfort, as all in-groups believe that "such ideas and opinions" are not supposed to come from *within* their own group. We say these things to others who appear as we do perhaps more in hope and fear than with any certain affirmation that this is in fact the case. This example brings us full circle to the opening of this chapter.

    The remainder of this volume will analyze several pairs of concepts that are often confused and collapsed in the same manner of those we have seen in the preceding. To do so leads us on both a personal and a social journey into the heart of our most cherished values, and puts at risk the facades by which we attempt to give meaning to a wider world that often remarks upon us negatively, if at all. It also exposes paths by which the mortal pilgrim of the day to day can overcome the nausea of rejection and create a more humane way of life for all.

Moral and Ethical

SOME THREE decades ago, when I was in elementary school, I noted for the first time the odd contrast between something that seemed to be fair and just and yet at the same time it's opposite. Akin to many schools, this one had various hortatory or homily-laden plackets posted in various places in the hallways and in classrooms, playing their part in the continuing experiment of using rationalized institutions to accomplish the general socialization of each new generation of children. The one of interest here stood high above our heads near the main office and simply stated "Smile and the world smiles with you. Cry and you cry alone." On the face of it, especially for a child, this seemed quite contrary to the self-interested habits of behavior reaffirmed by parents and others to that point. Crying, after all, *did* get other people's attention, and whether or not they cried with you was quite a secondary and even irrelevant point. Yet this was indeed the underlying point of the signage. We were gradually being resocialized *not* to bother other people with our problems, whether real or apparent. Instead, the slowly evolving adult world, the "real" world of fully socialized human beings in mass society, was one in which feelings should not be worn on one's sleeve. "Keep it to yourself" was becoming the watch-phrase of the day, or "tell someone who cares," the latter phrase containing in its acid wit the more empirically minded suggestion that no one in fact does!

In our society, a smile typically calls forth another, as long as the first is bright and not leering, and good-natured and not an element of poking fun. A smiling world must mean a happy world, and so the another subtext to the sign is that we ourselves can be the instigators of moments of joy in the world, fully calculated rather than that which supposedly resides in children "by nature." Instead of the self-centered plaintiff of childhood, then, we were being admonished to practice a good for another, which would help accomplish the common good. Yet the shadowy side of such a homily is the rejection contained in the second sentence. It says to us, "Better not cry, or you will be isolated and even worse off than you had imagined yourself to be." The basic element of social control of children, found also in Christmas songs containing like phrases prefaced by the warning "better not," is here overshadowed by the sense that what adult feelings and emotions are must always tend to the emotional well-being of the community and should not generally contain that suite of emotions that would "bring it down," as it were. Bringing others down is seen as an act of not merely selfishness but of resentment and envy, jealousy and even hatred. Crying serves all of the darker purposes of human emotions, whilst smiling is a beacon of those on the lighter side.

Of course, like most things adults advertise to children, it contains only a partial truth at best. Perhaps such a message is most true when considered not from a moral standpoint or an ethical viewpoint, but from one that is merely empirical. I say *merely*, because as a simple description of the mostly anonymous life of the world as it is, the smiling versus crying homily is almost always correct. A smile elicits its kindred, and while crying may promote concern, it is strangely not as immediately empathetic, mainly because in order for it to be so, it must call up similarly uncomfortable feelings within ourselves. We who are also socialized with this sense of conserving one's darker emotions for the common good and for social control do not desire to burst into tears, especially in public, just because someone else does. This thought leads us to one final note of the meaning of the signage in question. Even if we do begin to cry with another, we are still crying alone, because we do not know the meaning or intent of the others' tears, nor are they privy to ours, just through the act of emotion involved. We must communicate much more to have true empathy. Apparently this is not the case with smiling joy, or if it is, one is able to look beyond this and pretend it not to be so. Indeed, smiling sincerely without malice—though not necessarily without desire, attraction, or mirth—could be seen as part of the world of pretense more generally, a world in which we perform as if all was fine and under control.

The view of the "okay world," as Berger puts it, where all is not merely fine in the sense of "I'm alright Jack" and "Blue skies, shining at me," but also where all is *just,* and this not merely in the sense of "life may not be fair, but it is unfair to all of us at some time or other," but more profoundly, that way in which human life is lived cannot be but just because we are "human, all too human," is what we can call here the *moral* view of the world.

Although often confused and used in the same phrase, morals and ethics are very different and, in most ways, opposed to one another. How can this be so? Morality presents to us a set of principles that are supposed to be good for all times and places, like the Decalogue for example, where apparently obvious dicta such as "Thou shalt not kill" occur. Such declarations, sometimes in the form of *proscriptions* or taboos—you should not be doing this or that—and sometimes taking the form of *prescriptions* or exhortations—you should be doing this or that—are transparent to us because they both seem necessary for social control and for preventing the breakdown of community. Yet as well, they are presented as eternal truths or goods in themselves, no matter whether or not every member of society was by "human nature" in fact above such actions. The fact that we are manifestly not above them makes them ring all the more true to us. Yet it is this second characteristic of moral codes and their declarations that is shown by that self-same human history and experience to be faulty, or at least limited. Admitting the instrumentality of morals without evaluating them as goods or their opposite is both empirically and sociologically correct. Different sets of morals emanate from different societies, and they are not necessarily translatable into one another. Neither of these facts is fatal to the metaphysical idea of morality—that moral principles are eternal and perhaps even originate in a non-human transcendental realm, the realm of God or the gods, say. What shows up morality to be quite different than its claims to universality would wish for it is the sobering ambiguity of the human condition. Moral rules are *not* in fact good for all times and places, and our modern view is to see them as sourced in historical and very human contexts. Often these contexts are quite different from our own, so that we cannot perhaps even imagine how people must have lived in these other times and places. We begin to see morality as a template, a model for ideal behaviors but one that must be adjusted on a case-by-case basis depending on many other variables, much like jurisprudence adjusts the legal code and sets precedent both for it and against it from time to time. It is just at this point, when we are denuded of our metaphysical longings concerning morality and our desires to have some certain basis upon which all human life can take place within the good and thereby construct the good society, that ethics appears on our horizons.

This view is not merely modern. It was Aristotle who "invented" ethics, as it were, when he attempted to negotiate the notions of conduct and that of virtue. In so doing, the trial separation of ethics from metaphysics was begun. It is an unfinished project, mainly because within the space of ethics we still adhere to notions of *good* and *bad*, though these ideas are now not seen as ultimate and unchanging, like corresponding moral notions of *good* and *evil* used to be. It is not surprising that the term *evil* has fallen out of casual use and can be applied only to the most heinous of events in recent history, such as the Holocaust. The preservation of such a term allows it to hold some of its original weight, the chaos of malificence, which in our times became unutterably systematized. More than this, however, the notion of *bad* carries no ultimate weight when compared with that of *evil*, and this is how it should be, given that the spectrum of good and bad is an ethical one, and not strictly moral, as is good and evil. For once again, ethics is about the ongoingness of life in the world as it presents itself to us, and not about eternal principles that ideally are said to stand above such a world. The notion of a rule that is to be enacted and observed throughout the diversity of human contexts and conditions is a naive one. Instead, such changing situations must be understood and not "known." As the philosopher of the twentieth century, Hans-Georg Gadamer, reminds us, "Understanding plays a role wherever rules cannot simply be applied, and this includes the entire sphere of collective human life." (Gadamer 1996:165) Living is much more of a process than a result, and such ends as there may be within life are ultimately always yet more means.

Yet the dual nature of human knowledge in Western consciousness has the mark of eternal awareness to it. It is always sage to note that the "tree of knowledge" that appears as the symbolic augur of one of the fateful shifts in the human career in Hebrew mythic narrative is not merely a tree of knowledge per se but of the knowledge of good and evil. Right from the beginning then, in our recapitulation of even more ancient events—in this case the radical alienation from pre-agrarian subsistence patterns and their anthropologically well-known lifestyles of leisure and abundance and the beginning of the ethic of "work or die"—suggests to us that what we can know is never truly "value neutral." By this I mean that knowing something is to know it within the human context of values and evaluation, and that knowledge is good for something or else it is not. What that *something* is, is of course human life itself. Not only this, but mirrored in the distinction between morals and ethics is that such knowledge as it may be may change its value over time, and hence understanding rather than applying is the true order of the day for mortal beings with a finite consciousness. The duet of good and bad ends, ever coming in and out of tune with our lives both personal and cultural, is replicated in our attempts to build the good society, and in our notions of what might be good for most or all, or the inverse. The idea that human knowledge can never be ultimately value neutral and must always take on some working sense of either good or evil—or, most often and more realistically, a mixture of both; hence these moral notions are once again transformed into the ethical ones of good and bad—remains deeply imbedded in us. The great sociologist Emile Durkheim suggests that it is indeed part of our "nature":

> A belief that is as universal and permanent as this cannot be purely illusory. There must be something in man that gives rise to this feeling that his nature is dual, a feeling that men in all known civilizations have experienced. Psychological analysis has, in fact, confirmed the existence of this duality: it finds it at the very heart of our inner life. (Durkheim 1973:151 [1914])

Of course, the nature spoken of here is very human, and there is no suggestion that moral notions and their manifestations as body and soul, waking and dreaming life, or even the ego and the libidinal forces of our shadowy interiors are genetic or are shared with any other animal. It is within specifically "human nature"—that paradoxical situation in which all of us share our collective birthright— that we must look for an understanding of our evaluation of ourselves and our knowledge.

One of the major differences between the moral life and that of ethics is indeed the location of morality in our collective sense of ourselves. Morals are, for Durkheim, what he called "social facts," characteristics of a reality that is created by and for humans. Social facts are as real as the forces of nature about which scientific facts are grouped, but are of a different kind of reality. They rest in shared meanings and are expressed in beliefs. They have much more authority over us than do the facts of science, which often seem remote and of unlikely relevance to our day-to-day situations. Rather, we rely heavily on the norms of the social environment, fully assuming without much questioning and reflection that others will do the same, and society will "function" in a way with which we are both familiar and comfortable. That we become creatures of *habitus*, that is, what is customary, routine and correct in our lives, is not so much something to feel ashamed or critical of, but is in fact something necessary for human society in all of its forms. Not merely in order to reproduce what this or that culture takes to be important, but to reproduce humanity as a collective and sacred enterprise, is the demand to which habitus responds. Thus morality, as a social fact in each respective society and enacted through the habitus of its respective membership, is not generally up for negotiation nor even reflection. Not that it becomes manifest in our lives in an entirely transparent manner. It is rather its opacity—

Moral and Ethical

we feel its presence without quite being able to identify its source, like all other major forms of our early socialization—that gives it its relatively insulated status and to which we seem to voluntarily bend our individual wills.

What is moral then is not constructed in the same manner as what is ethical. The dialogue undertaken in the sphere of ethics looks more like a confrontation when we encounter the moral sphere. Durkheim explains this tension in this way:

> Although they are our own, they speak in us with a tone and an accent that are entirely different from those of our other states of consciousness. They command us; they impose respect on us; we do not feel ourselves to be on an even footing with them. We realize that they represent something within us that is superior to us. (ibid.:161)

Given that we encounter the moral sphere in a variety of ways in the day to day, from the apparently sacral profundity of a religiously inspired rite such as a marriage or a funeral, to the way certain commodities or services must be publicly displayed or advertised, such as alcohol or sexual pursuits, to the manner in which we disdain the marginal such as the street person or the prostitute, all reinforce the sense that morals are not at all about ourselves as individual thinking beings but rather characterize the reality of the world we all live in. It is also increasingly easy to understand why such tenets and their manifestations would be subject to rationalization. The social fact of morality in our lives is already and always a general convenience, whatever specific annoyances we might suffer with it if we wish to temporarily transgress it in some self-centered manner or on behalf of a special interest group. The pricking of conscience most of us feel when we have made ourselves into hypocrites for flaunting morality on the one hand in our private transactions yet stolidly defending its graces in public, is also usually a temporary setback to habitus. Morals are useful—this is why most scholars imagine them to be still present in their specific forms—and it is clear when we look at the careers of various historical moralities, that they, akin to their gods, come and go as they become more or less useful for other social invention and organization. Yet this is not the entire story. Many ideas which adhere to, or stem from, morality appear to defy the convenient efficiency of the rational utility of our day. Indeed, their presence confounds us more times than not, and seems to divide society rather than uphold the collective functional enterprise that morality supposedly represents. The apparently less useful moral notions are probably suffering slow shipwreck on the ever-changing coastline of historical trend. With his usual dubious wit, the geneticist and science educator Richard Dawkins gives a proverbial example, with the express motive to suggest to us that the source of much morality in our society is in fact immoral by the standards of its successors:

> God's monumental rage whenever his chosen people flirted with a rival god resembles nothing so much as sexual jealousy of the worst kind, and again it should strike the modern moralist as far from good role-model material. The temptation to sexual infidelity is readily understandable even to those who do not succumb, and it is a staple of fiction from Shakespeare to bedroom farce. But the apparently irresistible temptation to whore with foreign gods is something we moderns find harder to empathize with. To my naive eyes, "Thou shalt have no other gods but me" would seem an easy enough commandment to keep: a doddle, one might think, compared with "Thou shalt not covet thy neighbour's wife." Or her ass. (Or her ox.) Yet throughout the Old Testament, with the same predictable regularity as in bedroom farce, God had only to turn his back for a

moment and the Children of Israel would be off and at it with Baal, or some trollope of a graven image. (Dawkins 2006:243–44)

The stuff of anxious melodrama of what once were only oral narratives aside, what the real point of such allegories is simply that one must work to maintain a relationship with God and the morality that descends from Him. We find indeed this very language within subcultures that seek to reaffirm community and social order by ironically both rationalizing scripture to fit the needs of the day, while at once stepping outside mainstream forces of rationalization, whether or not these last come themselves from rational or nonrational sources. In our language, we must work to maintain a relationship of recognizable community and sociality, whatever the local source of this is presumed to be. Society indeed would falter fundamentally, and not in some mere local way, if our relationship with this or that morality became diffuse *as an ideal*. We will see that whenever the rubber of morality hits the road of lived experience, our relationship with it changes. Morality is transformed into an active ethics. But this does not mean that the moral sphere is jettisoned. We continue to refer to it, although now in this or that differing circumstance, we no longer automatically defer to it. Whatever we may think of the methods of communicating one of the essences of the social contract to marginal ethnicities several millennia ago, the principle of the message remains as important today as then. Turning one's back on what represents the entirety of the social bond—its rules, its commandments and structures, its gods—is to court disaster.

So much for the inertia of the predominance of morality in what could be seen as a predominantly nonmoral age. The content of the edicts have shifted to an extent for the majority of people in the developed world, whatever may have been the case for their ancestors, but the case *for* the continuing presence of morality remains.

The scene is quite different when one turns to what is to be considered ethical. The sense that ethics are morals enacted does not do this difference justice. The enactment of a moral as a principle, true to itself as an ideal, would never bend itself to the vagaries of the human condition as lived. At least since Aristotle, we have in fact constructed an alternate realm. The ethical takes place when we are unsure how to act or think. The ethical presents to us an inconvenience when compared with the application of a rule. We must "figure it out," as it were, rather than following what has been prefigured. Much of our respective socialization is a lengthy experiment in figuring out the world of social facts. This is a necessary bridge to the world where these facts become diffuse and diverse. The perspective of the structure of social relations allows us to see where and when we and others depart from it; when we begin to imagine a metaphorical tryst with another God. When we are thrown out into the world as it is, relatively unprotected by the institutions of socialization like family and school, and for some, the church, and relatively assaulted by other institutions—media, bureaucracy, work organizations, governments, the university for some, others' families and churches, perhaps—it is then that we realize that what we know is not enough. Coming to such sudden knowledge in itself is perhaps half the challenge, but the challenge of what to do and think in the face of the world stays with us for the remainder of our lives.

Even then we may feel we have little enough control over such decisions as might have to be made. Gadamer's biographer, the philosopher Jean Grondin, summarizes part of the former's thinking to this regard:

> Human understanding, behavior, feelings, love (for we do not comport ourselves to the world only, or primarily, in a cognitive way) have much less to do with consciousness, making, and control, and much more with unknowingly being inducted into the rituals of life, into a sequence of events that comprehends us and that we can spell out only stammeringly. The rituals in which life is enigmatically embedded represented much less of a limitation than an enabling condition of human reasonableness and feeling. (Grondin 2003:318)

The routines of life which often pass without comment contain in fact both occasions for our freedom and our imprisonment, and become charters for our habits of both doing and thinking. In this way morals maintain their relationship with ethics as a kind of mentoring. Morals say to us, "Remember, this is what one is supposed to do, see what can be done in light of this." Within each new social context, our previous prejudices shape our reactions. Only a radically new experience can tell us otherwise than what we have known, and most personal and social change occurs gradually, with the impetus and inertia of a slow buildup of smaller shifts in experience.

More recently, in his imposing volume *A Secular Age*, Canadian philosopher Charles Taylor sets out to chart the history of the relationship of morality and modern thought in the light of forces of rationalization and tradition. At a broad social level, and encompassing much of Western thinking, Taylor describes a reciprocating and symbiotic relationship between what we take as ideas of our own times and what we feel are ideas from our sometimes distant ancestors. Morality that is recognizable to us today as somehow old-fashioned, traditional, or as having some metaphysical source such as God or the gods, adheres to us from the ages of agricultural civilizations. Doing what we take to be "our own thing" in the face of this history—making history for ourselves as often against tradition as using it let alone being merely compelled by it—we take to be more along ethical lines. Ethical, because we feel that this is now "good for us," as well as flattering ourselves with the metaphoric pat on the back that says "well, good for you, good for us." Taylor suggests that we cannot become too naive about the apparently liberating effects of such a process, especially regarding rationalization, which, as we have already stated above, as often emanates from nonrational thinking as from rational. Such a process, which we often associate with human freedom in the face of oppressive structures of past social life, is itself structure anew, and cannot be otherwise:

> At this point, we become aware in the earlier play of code and negation that we are in danger of losing sight of. All structures need to be limited, if not suspended. Yet we cannot do without structure altogether. We need to tack back and forth between codes and their limitation, seeking the better society, without ever falling into the illusion that we might leap out of this tension of opposites into pure anti-structure, which could reign alone, a purified non-code, forever. (Taylor 2007:54)

In times of revolution or smaller crises of faith in what codes had ordered social life, there is often a euphoria that tells us that we can be free of all codes. Of course, following the heady events and thoughts of such momentary periods in history, there is always a combination of a return to the older codes just now disdained coupled with an admixture of perhaps once shocking ideas. This "new and improved" lot of thinking and acting becomes codified as social life again becomes routine, and habitus reappears on the social scene. Along with this, what once was shameful, immoral, or even from time to time disgusting, comes back for a curtain call, as it were, but the curtain never quite falls all the way. Taylor suggests that the "playing of the game" of what it means to be civil continues in an altered fashion:

Moral and Ethical

> ... civilization is a game we play together, relating to each other through disengaged persona, and thus maintaining the standards; when we violate one of these tabus, we not only arouse disgust, but we feel terrible shame. Civilization is in a sense a matter of feeling shame in the appropriate places." (ibid:142)

In this manner we can begin to understand the too quick confrontation between what we would like to be today, and what we feel was the case for our ancestors, much of which we shudder at—and this not at all merely at the level of technology or quality of life, as in not wishing to live in an age prior to the invention of antibiotics or, more trivially, the photocopier. Rather, it is considered ethical today precisely to call into relentless questioning the morals of our predecessors, whether or not they have a religious source. This is perhaps the major way in which the relationship between morals and ethics plays itself out. Taylor speaks of one of the results of this premature confrontation, using the cases where individuated spirituality confronts institutional religious authority:

> ... that this kind of question by its very nature must gravitate towards immanent self-concern, is an illusion which arises from the often raucous debate between those whose sense of religious authority is offended by this kind of quest, on the one hand, and the proponents of the most self- and immanent-centred forms, on the other, each of which likes to target the other as their main rival. "Look what happens when you abandon proper authority" (i.e., the Bible, or the Pope, or the tradition, according to the point of view), say the first; "don't you see that we alone offer an alternative to mindless authoritarianism," say the second. Each is comforted in their position by the thought that the only alternative is so utterly repulsive. (ibid:508–9)

We agree here that this is the most simplistic characterization of the confrontation with tradition, and hence the most naive. It immediately sets up a new tradition without either destroying the old one or incorporating its insights, such as they may be. By rejecting what has been the code but at the same time espousing a new code that can in its own way completely imprison us, we miss the entire point of the conversation that humanity has with its own history, one that we must replicate writ small in our own lives.

Like the proverbial two sides of the fence—it both keeps the other out but also keeps us in—the individuation of belief in spirituality, echoing the necessary translation of morals into more particular spaces of ethics, eventually may have the effect that the sphere of morality, with its mostly religious sources, is cast adrift on the ocean of "mere" history, or becomes a taboo by definition simply because it stems from "the tradition." No matter that the ostensible focus of the personal belief—an oxymoron for the social scientist given that a belief must be shared and socially reconstructed by successive generations—may be the God "Himself."

> The drive to a new form of religious life, more personal, committed, devoted; more christocentric; one which will largely replace the older forms which centred on collective ritual; the drive moreover, to wreak this change for everyone, not just certain religious elites; all this not only powers disenchantment... and new disciplines of self-control, but also ends up making the older holistic understandings of society less and less believable, even in the end nigh incomprehensible. (ibid:541)

Akin to Durkheim long before, Taylor reiterates the functional argument for the continuance of a certain kind of religion that not only issues morality but *enacts* it. Yet did we not just say that morality in action has to become ethics?

Yes, this is so in lived experience of the day to day, during which we participate in the habitus of the routine but also during which unexpected things might occur to us, forcing us to rewrite our prior prejudices in the face of the Sudden. The enactment of ritual in religion is rather like a controlled laboratory experiment in science. The variables and always altering social contexts of the day to day in the mundane (but potentially unpredictable) sphere are controlled for by the traditional acts of the ritual space. Within rituals of all kinds that adhere to traditional institutions in society, what is being sacralized is actually the time that is being lived and how it is being lived. Nothing should break in on us here. Even the call to the audience or congregation—really a rhetorical call to all others in the society—that if anyone wishes to not see this or that union or marriage take place they "should speak now or forever hold their peace," is a nod to the ritualizing effect of these sacral social contexts. All contexts are social, of course, but some are more intensely so than others. It is these somehow sacred times "out of time" as it were, that remind us in true Durkheimian fashion of the once collective conscience of this or that human group. There is even a space for the naysayer, but this space is demarcated and expected, even though, as is also to be expected, hardly anyone ever does offer an indignant veto to the happy couple and their families. Yet in spite of this, the call is not mere rhetoric. We are aware in this space, more than in those more routine, that the intensity of society and of our participation in it brings to the surface other feelings that hint at or even will its negation. These more shadowy feelings on our parts are diffuse in mundane circumstances, and are also made less threatening to social order in general precisely because the day-to-day life is the space of ethical decisions, and ethics are inherently open-ended, giving us the appearance that our qualms about participating "properly" in the social "game" could engage in renegotiating it. Not so in the realm of ritual. Because this realm is of the moral essence and the presence of moral enactments is in fact a counter-threat to these qualms or doubts, suspicions or criticisms, these latter rise the more violently to conscious thought and elicit the corresponding emotions.

All of this Taylor seems to miss, but he does identify at least two of the results of this rebellion against the veracity of moral norms and respective sacral theaters. That is, we imagine that we can thrust upon the social world our own sense of what morals ought to be. Once again, we already *do* this through the use of ethical reflection, but this time such an "ought" itself claims moral status whereas in fact it really has none:

> What is striking [is this] claim to issue the norms we live by on our own authority. This thought can set off a tremor, a frisson in us, as we sense how much we are defying an age-old sense of higher, more-than-human authority; and at the same time, it can galvanize us with a sense of our own responsibility, and the courage we need to take it up. Beyond this, we can be struck by the sense that we stand, as it were, before a normative abyss, that this blind, deaf, silent universe offers *no* guidance whatever; we can find here an exhilarating challenge, which inspires us, which can even awaken a sense of the strange beauty of this alien universe, in the face of which we stake our claim as legislators of meaning. (ibid:581; italics in the original)

The modern reality of the void or "abyss of meaning" certainly is an occasion for ethics to shine. If now morals are in fact mute, or at best bear their mute testimony to us through the memorializations we give them in our collective rituals—the old jest about the likeness of weddings and funerals may be seen as a remarking upon this awareness—then it is we who have individual life experience who must speak both in and to the cosmos which is radically not of ourselves. In the moral vision, the circle of life in pre-agricultural social organizations, and the cycle of the harvest in agrarian societies, spoke their entire volume within a closed shape. As Taylor suggests, this form of life is epitomized in its circumference, but we today are much more painfully aware, it seems, that we cannot ever close that circle, at least not within the mortal species that we are at present. Instead, we must avoid imagining that closure and then marketing it as the true and final answer to all things living and ambiguous:

> So religious faith can be dangerous. Opening to transcendence is fraught with peril. But this is particularly so if we respond to these perils by premature closure, drawing an unambiguous boundary between the pure and the impure through the polarization of conflict, even war. That religious believers are capable of this, history amply attests. But atheists as well, once they open themselves to strong ideals, such as the republic of equals, a world order of perpetual peace, or communism. We find the same self-assurance of purity through aggressive attack on "axes of evil", among believers and atheists alike. Idolatry breeds violence. (ibid:796)

What appear to be the highest ideals—none more grotesque than the Nazi aesthetic "philosophy" of beautifying the world through violence—are often put into action by the most horrifying behaviors. The world itself does not tolerate intolerance. Any set of ideals, adored to the exclusion of the ever-opening ambiguity of human meaning—what are our ultimate ends, both in the sense of purpose and demise, for example—becomes a set of idols, ready to backdrop the worst in ourselves.

There are institutions, however, that mitigate this historical tendency. Given that it is unlikely that the adoration of idols comes from a nonhuman source, we have also invented sets of ideals that attempt to mirror more realistically the vagueness of life. Sagan mentions the legal system of certain nation-states as theoretically in place to complete the official translation of morality into ethics, and thus dispense justice rather than dispensing with it: "A kind of cost-benefit analysis is made. The guilty may on occasion be set free so that the innocent will not be punished. This is not only a moral virtue, it also inhibits the misuse of the criminal-justice system to suppress unpopular opinions or despised minorities. It is part of the error correction machinery." (Sagan 1996:431) This rather formalized version of the day-to-day decision-making in which we are all involved simply holds the entire process up for wider public scrutiny. Reality should not be made into a cult, says this understanding of the human condition. Given this, the loose threads of our moral tapestry are those we must tolerate and police in a balanced manner. Both the great American pragmatist philosopher William James and Durkheim suggest that the extremities of society—often made manifest in its artists, saints, and leaders of other kinds—are present to help the normative life that is the lot of the rest of us ordinary mortals be more tolerable. Not only this, their example serves to help us pull ourselves up toward their ideals by our own bootstraps. They are a reminder of what human talent can become. Yet they also often go wrong enough in our eyes to force us to limit their genius lest it destroy the civility and, ironically as well, the space of ethical translation that allows their perspective to be felt as relevant. Speaking specifically of great artists such as Brecht and Pound, but using their cases only as examples of this general point, the social philosopher Hannah Arendt reminds us that the peaks and valleys of human accomplishment often appear side by side in the same person:

Moral and Ethical

> The chronic misbehavior of poets and artists has been a political, and sometimes a moral, problem since antiquity.... I shall stick to the two assumptions I have mentioned. First, although in general Goethe was right and more is permitted to poets than to ordinary mortals, poets, too, can sin so gravely that they must bear their full load of guilt and responsibility. And, second, the only way to determine unequivocally how great their sins are is to listen to their poetry—which means, I assume, that the faculty of writing a good line is not entirely at the poet's command but needs some help, that faculty is granted him and that he can forfeit it. (Arendt 1968:218)

It is not merely on principles of mediocrity that we push the extremities amongst us to live as we must. It is we, indeed, who know what an extremity is, given that we so seldom encounter it, for good or evil, in our own lives. Rather, we are encountered *by* it, and if this seems an odd turn of phrase, consider the existentialist philosopher Martin Heidegger's comment about the dual effect of both the weight of history that lies on us, as Marx reiterated, "like a dead hand upon the living," but also the simultaneous fact that we write our own lives through their living: "History hits us, and we are history itself." The artist, saint, philosopher, or leader of some other stripe seems to step outside of this intense dual focus of historical forces and looks back down upon it, allowing the genius to comment as if they were a third eye. But, of course, ultimately this cannot be so. The artist is as human as the rest of us, as the history of artists' foibles and flaws so painfully shows us. All the more so, these weaknesses show up as great blights across an otherwise noble palette, and the abilities of our palates to distinguish between their acts of good and evil is thereby heightened. We are forced to act, and thence to judge

> However, the equality before the law whose standards we commonly adopt for moral judgements as well is no absolute. Every judgement is open to forgiveness, every act of judging can change into an act of forgiving; to judge and to forgive are but the two sides of the same coin. But the two sides follow different rules. The majesty of the law demands that we be equal—that only our acts count, and not the person who committed them. The act of forgiving, on the contrary, takes the person into account; no pardon pardons murder or theft but only the murderer or the thief. (Arendt 1968:248)

Whether we are placed on the side that judges or that which forgives, we must evaluate our actions and our beings with the perspective of both. "Mitigating circumstances" on the side of judgment are usually taken to be the acts of others, or the effects of structural forces beyond the control of those whom we must judge, such as the happenstance of an unfortunate birth. The presumed character or even "nature" of the individual person is the source of mitigation on the side of forgiveness. Of course, we have given unto all of the gods of history and culture these abilities that we as humans need to maintain the social contract with each other. We cannot let things get too out of hand, and if this statement sounds at first too conservative, it is better thought of as conserving, that is, keeping in place what we know to have been viable before. We also know—though no doubt many of us conspire to suppress this fact—that what has gone before is also indeed gone and thus cannot be trusted to steer us right in the present. Thus the legal system is a kind of hall of mirrors, keeping up the pretense that we knew what we were doing then and can continue to know now if we only hold the course. Ultimately, this cannot be so, and the presence of the human extremes and their actions in the form of artists or whoever reminds us that what has been moral cannot be what now must be ethical:

It was an implicit admission that the past spoke directly only through things that had not been handed down, whose seeming closeness to the present was thus due precisely to their exotic character, which ruled out all claims to binding authority. Obligative truths were replaced by what was in some sense significant or interesting, and this of course meant... that the "consistence of truth... has been lost." (Arendt 1968:195)

Perhaps it was inevitable that our worldview not only finally recognize that the ambiguity of living presents an intractable situation for the mere application of rules. Not only the fetish about following the rule or surrounding "policy and procedure" would be resultant of this, but also, and in contradistinction to this, the loss of any objective background for the rules themselves to hang their hats on. On the one hand, we are compelled to adhere to rules for their own sake. This adoration is, on the other hand, only the compulsion all once lovers feel when they would long to love again but have not a reason to do so. We learn this social tension at an early age, and learn that we must cope with it as best we can: "Often the children, unaware that they have rights to friendship, understanding or agreeable play—unaware, indeed, that the adults would be greatly interested in such matters—suffer in silence and submit to the intolerable." (Riesman 1950:69) The primary reason why we adults show a distinct lack of interest in many social relationships and even emotions that would ideally be regarded as not merely civil but human a right is that we do not wish to be reminded that we had lost them at an early age. This situation may be compared with other kinds of communities more similar to those previously mentioned as "mechanical" More importantly, Riesman's classic analysis of North American society reminds us that "For the individual in a society dependent on tradition-direction has a well-defined functional relationship to other members of the group. If he is not killed off, he 'belongs'—he is not 'surplus,' as the modern unemployed are surplus, nor is he expendable as the unskilled are expendable in modern society." (ibid:12) Similar to the sense we have that rules can stand without morals, and that the presence of ethics, above all, testifies to the lack of truth in human activities—rather than to the profound truth of their ambiguity and thus the necessity to refer to morality without automatically deferring to it—the moral weight of having expendable human beings is shrugged off as a piece of ethical detritus. Really, all of us are potentially expendable in our day and age, and this is a function of a mode of production that has outgrown the need for specific specialists who cannot be replaced by another like them, or, increasingly, with a machine.

We are not heedless of this quandary, but we respond to it in a perverse manner. The most developed societies in terms of industry and technology, use of resources, and production of commodities usually have the most developed social networks of welfare, health, and education. The two sets of characteristics appear to go hand in hand. The price that much of the world continues to pay for these yet regional developments, however, must be the largest "human sacrifice" in history. We are long past the period where many children were needed to reproduce subsistence strategies and viable communities, and indeed, the birth rate in developed countries often falls below "replacement." That is, we often hear that we are "not having enough children" to replace ourselves—or for the next generation of production and consumption to sustain itself. We supplement this lack with immigration techniques, although these are quite specific. We do not want just anyone to carry on our legacy. Our rather proprietary feelings regarding capitalism and democracy have not prevented it from spreading to traditionally very different cultures, and in a sense we wish for that, because it corresponds mightily with the idea that we in fact do have

Moral and Ethical

the best society possible, as discussed in the previous chapter. Yet the ability or willingness to share this good with others unlike us is still severely limited. If these others can serve us in some way, then perhaps we can share something of our merits with them. If they wish to compete with us, or yet out-compete us, then we become quite hostile, even paranoid. What is true abroad is also true at home. Immigrants, if not left to their own devices, are encouraged in various ways to take up the marginal positions for which we have no use, due to their generally derogated status. From the point of view of the newcomer, our society appears to have only extremes. The privilege of wealth and apparent leisure are in contiguity with the person on the street, or the mentally ill, the addict, or the criminal. Not that these last three do not sometimes overlap with privilege, it is just that when they do, they can be hidden by wealth and networks having that which sociologists call "social capital." In order to preserve this privilege for ourselves, we remain interested in having and raising our own children, despite the great masses of expendable children in the world at large. Ominously, when children who look like us become available on the more or less open market of international adoption—the popular cases of abandoned orphanages full of Eastern European fair haired and blue-eyed girls is well-known here—we rush to secure their safety and succor. That these cases are rare and come with specific crises in culture we take to be kindred to our own only points up the apparent hypocrisy, perhaps downright ethnicism or even xenophobia, when we contemplate the implications of difference.

Consider what will at first seem Draconian and contrary to all moral feeling. What if, in order to pay heed to the theological philosopher Paul Ricoeur's remonstrance that "the love we have for our own children does not exempt us from loving the children of the world," we were *forced* to stop having our own children, perhaps temporarily? We generally feel that having our own child is a human right, ideally universal. Yet we deny this would-be right to most in the world, if that right includes, as it must, the humane quality of life that all children ideally should have as human beings. We cannot have it both ways, on the one hand denying this right to others while on the other preserving it for ourselves. So, what if some hypothetical social institution forced us to give up the apparent right to our own children unless and until *all* the children of the world were provided their full humanity? At the same time, we would force those others in their different worlds to stop having children for a time as well, to catch up, as it were. Now, is this "modest proposal" at all necessary or even ethical? Our way of doing things, modern industrial production, high technology and the wealth generated from it, does of course have the present capability, properly distributed, to look after all in round terms of health and material well-being. Marx imagined this was the case during the advent of capitalism, perhaps naively so. Would it not be better, then, to redistribute in the light of the moral weight of universal human rights? Given that we have shown the distinct lack of any will to do so unless forced by social policy—usually functioning best in the smallest of our democracies—the ethic of this imaginary social policy rests elsewhere. The loss of our own children forces us into empathy with the other who is currently losing theirs. Ethics itself is born of and borne on often radical changes in the way we see the world. Such shifting in our social location, Gadamer says, "… leads us again to the special kind of knowing that is *phronesis*, wisdom. Here we should formulate a basic principle or, if you will, a first proposition—*phronesis* is evidently the most important of all the developments of practical philosophy, of ethics; and one must further acknowledge that this was all there was in ethics at the outset…" (Gadamer 2004:78) In the case of masses of expendable humanity in a world where the ideals of a universal humanity are celebrated, the moral disjuncture is immediately intolerable. Wisdom in such a case would be to enact "... genuine communication through speech, conversation, sympathetic insight into the other, consensus, and, finally, respect for the other, which stands higher than love, since all love is really a kind of will to power." (ibid:58) Surely our current situation fundamentally lacks respect for the other and for the children of the other.

If we could feel as they must, or, ironically, as we would hope and expect them to feel in the face of their loss, would we not be more inclined to initiate an ethics that would alleviate both of our suffering? Ours, now that we have been forced into childlessness, and theirs in that their children are doomed often to a living death, is enough reality anew that we can enact our moral ideals in the service of a greater humanity. Once again, and yet with still further irony, this is what we desire to do anyway, through the spread of our religions, politics, and economies around the globe. We might be quite suspicious that by this time we do not really wish to share any of these things, but our "sharing" comes in the form of dominance over others and comes with the goal of preserving that dominance. The hypothetical loss of the vehicles by which such dominance continues and to which we hand it down would force us to reconsider profoundly what once was considered wise.

Of course we do have a current and often animated public debate regarding the necessity of children in North America. It takes the form of the concerns surrounding abortion, the rights of women, and the rights of the to-be, or already, human. The alternating views can be quite polarized, even violently so. The "pro-choice" side is called "pro-abortion" by its opposition, and the "pro-life" side is called "anti-choice" by theirs. Yet our hypothetical example is more truly "pro-abortion," as one might assume that the blanket ban on children would raise the abortion rate and in fact indirectly declare this to be ethical in the circumstance, though not moral in principle. All the better, our social critic suggests, as we as would-be parents would be torn from our fulfillments in ways that bring us closer to the great bulk of humanity who may indeed share our desires to this regard but must deal with risks that we have overcome, in part by foisting them on others. However this may be, most of us would feel automatically repelled by the idea that we should endure a Herod-like moratorium on childbearing. It is this repellence and revulsion, even felt as part of a thought experiment, which is important for us to grasp and attempt some empathetic understanding of less privileged others. Though there be likely no transcendental necessity for the reproduction of our species (and indeed, no local natural necessity either; the earth's biosphere would be much better off without us, especially the guise of ourselves succeeding the industrial revolution), we almost universally think that having children is in fact a human right, available to all. Our ability to reject the overturning of this right and the emotional level of our rejection of it links us with the mechanical societies of our ancient ancestors. For it is within the collective conscience that such values that appear instinctual to us rise in our consciousness and brook no debate. Our problem is that we have not yet learned to extend what is rightfully human to all of humanity, and by virtue of this oversight, in fact tend to delimit such rights of our "nature." We *do* favor our own children, and try to love them more in most cases, contrary to the moral dictum of Ricoeur. The overcoming of this parochiality will not take place through Herodian measures but through the widened ability to empathize with the marginal other. Thought experiments aside, personal experience of the other's plight might serve, even though the vast majority of us in North America will not have such experiences, unless we link losing our own children to natural circumstances such as disease to the general sense that others try to bring children into the world at grave risk. The affirmation of a universal right of "human nature" and the rejection of its delimitation shows the resonance of the "mechanical solidarity" that I spoke of earlier. Taylor draws attention to an alternate sense of this return to another "Durkheimian" time from our own age and, in spite of appearing to be conservatively apologetic for many things traditional and especially religiously inspired, ultimately suggests rejecting this return:

> Some conservative souls feel that it is sufficient to condemn this age to note that it has led great numbers into modes of free floating not very exigent spirituality. But they should ask themselves two questions: First, is it conceivable that one could return to a paleo- or even neo-Durkheimian dispensation? And secondly, and more profoundly, doesn't every dispensation have its own favoured forms of deviation? If ours tends to multiply somewhat shallow and undemanding spiritual options, we shouldn't forget the spiritual costs of various kinds of forced conformity: hypocrisy, spiritual stultification, inner revolt against the Gospel, the confusion of faith and power, and even worse. Even if we had a choice, I'm not sure we wouldn't be wiser to stick with the present dispensation. (Taylor 2007:513)

Yet we have all of these spiritual costs in today's society as well as those that we imagine harbored them in the past. No doubt we cannot go back, in any sense of the phrase. Our linear conception of time itself immediately denies this desire, even if we indeed ultimately do desire it. Because each generation privileges its own version of youth, and derogates the youth of the present—as is said, youth is, notoriously, "wasted on the young"—we in turn are open to imagining returns of various kinds. Memorialization presses these desires upon us, and the "good old days" are ubiquitous for those whose present life is fundamentally unfulfilling. The continuing reverberance and dynamism of sectarian religion in North America testifies to not only the desire for instant community, which these churches and their corresponding social movements provide for newcomers, but also the sense that a truer community can be found within them. The community of God's children is more rhetoric in these cases than anything substantial, but it does serve to pin a label on this sometimes suppressed and apparently vital need of many human beings to feel that they "belong" somewhere. It is not enough to belong to God as a solitary or alienated person, but for our mortal selves, we imagine we need God's presence on earth in the form of a human community. Finally, such movements serve as attempts to restore something deemed lost to us. Social order or, at least, the order that our once youth created for our now adult beings is apparently threatened with each generation anew, as our children take to the metaphorical streets of adolescence and burgeoning autonomy. Although we ourselves did the same, larger social structures impinged on us and forced our own revolutions to follow the path of all revolutions, retrogressing into a disappointingly only somewhat altered version of the society we rebelled against, all those years ago. Perhaps we are, ironically, now attached and loyal to these structures and orders and seek to defend them as they were once defended against ourselves. Perhaps we are, perversely, now resentful and jealous of younger people as they attack what now seems to be our own. Perhaps we are, ultimately, envious of youth in an existential way, as it has passed from the faces of our contemporaries, never to return.

So in not being able to go back, we defend what in our own history was once seen as indefensible. The challenge for each upcoming generation is then set as not in fact rebelling against social norms and forms but in understanding them in a better way than did previous generations. When the next generation takes them over as their own, a different understanding of them then mere artificial limits on "the good life" and on "freedom" will help our successors to change them more radically and more permanently, hopefully with the cause of a general humanity in mind.

> To affect the theater of going back is, however, not at all beyond us. It is in fact a regular occurrence in contemporary society. Yet there is a price to be paid for all theatrical visions, "For the fragility of these repeatedly restored props of the public order is bound to become more apparent after every collapse, so that ultimately the public order is based upon people's holding as self-evident precisely those 'best known truths' which scarcely anyone still believes in." (Arendt 1968:11)

We have seen that to confuse morals and ethics is to believe in the theatrical or ritual application of rules as if they were an unambiguous reflection and transparent description of the human condition. If society is to be more than a pretense, if we as individuals are to be more than "apes of our own ideals," to paraphrase Nietzsche, then we must learn to recognize that what is ethical at once refers to what is moral while at the same time appearing to betray it. Although this duet may be disconcerting for us, it is not more disconcerting than to either banally apply rules that can only be ideals or, worse, to pretend to uphold ideals and then practice their very opposite. Ethics are not the opposite of morals. They instead confront morality in the same way as living history confronts tradition. They are in dialogue with one another, and they participate in dialectic. The moral learns from the ethical, and the second critiques the first. These two fundamental processes occur simultaneously between morals and ethics. They are the same two processes that allow humanity to live and learn. We cannot be slaves to how others have lived, and yet we have much to learn from them. Neither can we support their being our servants, but we would yet hope that they would wish to respond to and respect our teachings if they could do so. Distinguishing between *moral* and *ethical* allows us to understand a relationship that many parents and their children come to know: that all knowledge and all things come to us in circles, and we cannot come to either examine or to know ourselves without walking with the other. In this way, we *can* affect a real return.

Prudence and Prudishness

ATTEMPTING TO make a good society, we rightly feel we need to hold on to the strides already made. Conserving the good implies that the good can be accumulated, and that one step leads to another along the same path to our ideals. Modern knowledge is taught in this manner, and particularly, the information and knowledge required in technical fields of applied science and the professions assume a cumulative step-by-step growth of acumen. Almost as if we were making up for the seeming happenstance and trial-and-error stumbling of our primary socializations—what all of us must learn as children and adolescents in order to function correctly in normative life—formal education rather militaristically indoctrinates us into the fields of "praxis." "Hexis," or what is customary, must give way to what is considered technical or even scientific knowledge on many fronts. It is well known that what science says to us is almost always contradictory, or at least different, from what the local knowledge of our upbringing says. More importantly, there does not seem to be any concept of duty with the former. With science, we can either take it or leave it, and not all of us need be interested in the discursive or technical enterprise it promotes. We have no such options regarding our birthright, the regional knowledge of our various cultural legacies. Here, we are fully expected to be loyal to what comes down to us semi-consciously and what we seem to learn through a kind of repetitive osmosis. Notions such as kindred, friendship, community, morality, and etiquette, to name a few, are all ensconced in this realm of the "native's point of view." Science claims to take us beyond this local vantage point, as its statements of "fact" are to be regarded as universally binding on all persons, all cultures, and even all times. Yet the word *binding* here is not at all the same as the duty or loyalty we feel toward our cultural backgrounds. Instead of being associated with honor, or filial piety, or moral scruples or even public civility, to be bound to the knowledge of science means to accept simply the way things are in nature and our place in it.

This alone is not radically new, as we have seen all of the agrarian religions that are still recognizable to us also let us know that there is an order to the universe and our ultimate place in it is fixed and immutable. We must have simply accepted this as well, if we were living in another time and place, the space of our ancestors. The real difference between the duty felt to any portion of our tradition, including religious cosmology, and the binding nature of modern scientific knowledge is that the order this latter presents to us is a *non-moral* one. Like its corollary spaces in rationalized organizations—politics, economics, formal education—science explains the cosmos as without a purpose that is without itself. That is, there is no significance to nature beyond what nature appears to be. Nietzsche famously mocked this new idea, though he was also using it to satire the half-baked attempts at rehabilitating it for morality, by reminding us that the difference between "real" and "apparent" had vanished with modern science. What is, is simply that and nothing more. Our understanding of our place in this new universe was thus suddenly bereft of the older and more local notions of loyalty and what it meant to be "bound" to a set of ideas or actions and social relationships. The purposeless cosmos—again, purpose being defined as something beyond its own existence and process—had no place for the significance of anything, including humans, beyond the probable or improbable outcomes of complex evolutionary crucibles. Just as the awesome seeming infinitude of the cosmos was made known to us through our new prosthetic devices of telescope and microscope and in turn made us feel, ironically, very local indeed, we also were by definition pushed into a place of insignificance. This smallness and irrelevance is not merely spatial and temporal. The universe is vast beyond human imagination and actual lifespan, and so is its timescale.

But again, the mere data of these facts is not enough to warrant the abandoning of purpose and sense of moral place. What science added was that the essence of the cosmos was that there was nothing aside from this tandem of voids. The traditional reasons for human life itself, let alone various local reasons to live a good life, were vanquished from powerful institutions of knowledge production. The seeming immorality of the nation-state and its politics rests in part on this transition, and the complaints often voiced about each new generation's moral vices participate in the same. We are aware, no matter what lengths we go to suppress or deny this knowledge, that we live in an abyss of meaning, or, at least within a relative paucity of the older meanings that gave humans purposes and reasons for everything for at least all of written history.

With the advent of the void, however awesome and beautiful we judge it to be—and one of the main interests in the Hubble space telescope it seems to me is the aesthetically gorgeous vistas it continuously presents to the human eye—we are left rather listlessly living alone. The tension between desiring meaningfulness as the reason for human life and the ultimate apparent meaninglessness of life itself give rise to the odd confluence of the two ideas discussed in this chapter. Both prudence and prudishness arise out of the tension between traditional values, whatever their diverse but unscientific cultural locations and origins, and the apparently valueless space of science. Certainly, science also demands that we be cautious in our explorations of nature, and this caution is not most profoundly the stuff of "science fiction" melodramas such as Star Trek, where intrepid humans "go where no one has gone before," often at their peril. More importantly, the scientific method tells us that we must not only curb or bracket our cultural expectations, desires, and dreams in the use of our imagination to formulate research questions and link existing data into explanation, but that we, in observing nature, must be cautious not to make that observation into self-fulfilling prophecy. These cautions ring true both within the scientific process itself and when science is put to use in the world of the day to day. As stated, we notoriously, "accept the products of science while rejecting its methods," and hence the nub of the problematic confusion between prudence and prudishness.

One might well wonder why it is the rejection of scientific method that is the source of this modern conflation. Does not prudishness rather call to mind some kind of latter-day Puritanism, especially regarding sexuality? Does not prudence rather express a general caution more associated with public behavior and even etiquette? These are reasonable queries to raise at this point. To be prudish is almost always seen as a foible, if not an outright character deficiency, and the topic is almost always a moral one, not a scientific one. To be prudent is generally seen as a positive trait, if not a moral virtue. Yet both of these concepts bring themselves to bear in the face of the new, whether it be general experience, cross-cultural others, ideas concerning nature and our place in it, and sometimes even new technologies and their application. This last category in particular sparks the tension between to the two concepts. Stem cells are a risk as are electric cars, but for different reasons. The first impinges upon our moral order, the second upon our economic system. But the best defense against changes of all sorts enlists both the caution of the pragmatist in prudence as well as the caution of the moralist in prudishness. The voicing of these lines of defense have taken on a ritual and predictable character, and our part of a larger theater that Taylor suggests has become a necessary part of our society:

> The public sphere is a central feature of modern society. So much so, even where it is in fact suppressed or manipulated it has to be faked. Modern despotic societies have generally felt compelled to go through the motions. Editorials appear in party newspapers, purporting to express the opinions of the writers, offered for the consideration of their fellow citizens; mass demonstrations are organized, purporting to give vent to the felt indignation of large numbers of people. All this takes place as though a genuine process were in train of forming a common mind through exchange, even though the result is carefully controlled from the beginning. (Taylor 2007:185–86)

Earlier, the concept of "civility" had become so important as to permit it to become a mere charade in social organizations of all forms aspiring to "civilization" (ibid:100). An ordered social sphere in a mass society appears to need ways in which the inevitable desires and anxieties of persons can be expressed without ever truly or radically endangering what we all take for granted. The irony here is of course that our sense of a need for change rests on the very thing we want changed, or at least a part of it. We assume things can change while at the same time assuming things are not going to change, even though they could. At the same time, in some other portion of the public sphere, we assume things will not change even if we wanted them to, and yet further, in some other part, we assume that things will never change in large part because we do *not* want them to do so. This potent mix of conflicted and sometimes even contrary desires suggests the best course of action to those who manage the nation-state's official apparatus and to those who write and re-write its official histories, that the theater of change and its dynamic should become an artifact, lest all social order cease to be viable. For some, the only way to counter the weight of the state in the *polis* is to return to the moral sphere and make *that* public, in a real sense resurrecting the previous form of large-scale authority, that traditional, in the face of the modern rational-legal kind.

This means a return to the most dominant historical source of moral discourse—that is to say, religion. Religion can aid us in offering both kinds of resistances to change. Whether this is warranted or not scientifically is quite a secondary question, although often enough—as in the case of the ecumenical environmental lobbies—these erstwhile competitors do come together. What really is prudish can be cast as prudence, and what may have in fact no real moral scruple based in previous forms of etiquette and given form in modern diagnostics of neuroses of various, usually sexual, kinds, can take the form of mere pragmatic caution, which any "sane and civil" human being would recognize as a public virtue. When this occurs,

> ... religious discourse will be very much in the public sphere. Democracy requires that each citizen or group of citizens speak the language in public debate that is most meaningful to them. Prudence may urge us to put things in terms which others relate to, but to require this would be an intolerable imposition on citizen speech. As the sense of living in Christendom fades, and we recognize no spiritual family is in charge, or speaks for the whole, there will be a greater sense of freedom to speak our own minds,

and in some cases that will inescapably be formulated in religious discourse. (ibid:532)

The loss of the language of religion is not what it appears to be. It indeed reappears with more vitality and in a more vociferous manner than before when it was merely assumed to take care of things "on its own," as it were. Now the moral order must be defended against heretical changes emanating from nonmoral or even amoral sources. The former would include science and would merit a prudent reaction. The latter would include all those areas of modern life that transgress older boundaries of good behavior in both public and private spheres and thus would garner the more prudish reaction. It is easy to see how the two reactions, serving a common front, can become confused. This confusion could also be calculated by the rearguard. Deliberate confusion of prudence and prudishness enfranchises both the pragmatic mind and the moral. The former speaks to our sense of usefulness—do we really need to be studying black holes and the origin of the cosmos when there are so many people starving?—and the latter speaks to our sense of what is right and proper—no sex please, but if you have to you must at least face the consequences (of childbearing, disease, or stigmata directed at deviant practices). The combination of these concepts is often seen as a necessary one, although not entirely ingenuous, because of the sheer blanket force of the very much disingenuous agents for "apparent" changes to society:

> On another level, the "atonal banshee of emerging egomania" unavoidably impinges through the ubiquity of advertising and the entertainment media, insistently calling us each to our own satisfaction and fulfillment, linking the powerful forces of sexual desire and the craving for wholeness, constitutive elements of our humanity, to products promoted to the status of icons, and in the

process obscuring, emptying, and trivializing these forces themselves. (ibid:552)

Taylor summarizes Marx's indictment of what the latter famously called "commodity fetishism," where the original religious characteristics of the fetish are transformed into those secular. Reliquary to archive, veneration to adoration, aura to glamour and the like populate the list of changes, and in fact resonate with the same feared changes to come that some of us wish to defend against. As well, the proliferation of forms of commodity to be fetishized and the technical genius needed to create them is bewildering and contrary to our older expectations that one moral surface is both the path to righteousness and to salvation:

> As a result, the consumer, in his leisure pursuits, meets vastly increased standards of technical competence. These increase his anxiety about his ability as a consumer. He can no longer evaluate the work, the artistry of the performer, by reference back to the working sphere of his own life. (Riesman 1950:158)

The reaction is to very often throw up one's hands and say, "I guess anything goes, these days!" Commenting on society and ourselves, we ask, "Is nothing sacred?" Abortion, stem cell research, cosmogony—the narrative of the birth and development of the universe, lately taken over by science—the discovery of the elements of organic life on other solar bodies and the weekly discovery of extra-solar planets—those which orbit stars other than our own—could all be rather disconcerting to the idea that there is a fixed sacred and its contents alone are those to be deemed moral.

Even the most capable minds may become prudent in the face of both the guttural quality of commodities and their marketed fetishes coupled with the overwhelming knowledge of the cosmos as infinite and anonymous. Grondin relates how Gadamer in coming to North America, found that "Other solidarities—the Puritan heritage of social communitarianism, among others—are very much alive. Traditions are often superior to science, he taught." (Grondin 2003:319) As well, if we rely only on those with the most political power in society, we are at risk of being disenfranchised if we do not offer wholehearted public support to their desires: "Every exclusion from this group that decides our fate means a loss of the future." (ibid:156) Much earlier in his life, the great philosopher encountered in his mentor, Heidegger, the key difference between prudence and what would become manifest only as the prudish:

> Making an even stronger impression on Gadamer than the 1923 class was the seminar on the *Nichomachean Ethics*, where Heidegger perplexed his listeners by identifying the practical virtue of *phronesis* (prudence) with conscience, which calls us back to ourselves. Suddenly *phronesis* did not have to do with the antiquated *prudentia*, enshrined in the church's catalogue of virtues; instead, it was concerned with the life-changing decision of those whose being was continually put at risk. (ibid:106)

Indeed, when faced with any kind of change in our lives, we employ an odd combination of pragmatism and moralism. We ask ourselves on these occasions, and more pressingly when the changes are imagined as fundamental, whether or not we can use them and improve our quality of life, as well as whether or not they are *good* for us, that is, whether or not we become better people than we were if we accept the change. This tandem of self-examination in the light of the world is a necessary one. How it gets confused occurs when we become prematurely defensive in the face of potential change. We have something to lose, we imagine, or we are insecure about our ability to make the change, or we are arrogant about the superiority of our present self versus that which may appear after proceeding with the change.

There is also the present-day problem of imagining that we are as existential beings as rule-bound as the world appears to be. The habits and routines of everyday life confide in us an artifice: We are what we are only if we follow as others do. If we transgress the boundaries of the day to day, we become some other person, something quite different from who we actually are. But this is a fallacy. Social norms present themselves as guidelines for correct public, and sometimes private, behavior. If the latter is to remain private, for example, it too must not be too extreme. We are aware that there are consequences for transgression, but that these consequences, too, are social constructions, the rearguard reactions of a sociality displaced, momentarily, by the creativity or careless activities of the individual. We accept these and perhaps some of us even relish their challenge to us as free persons who confront them in our authenticity. Either way, by voluntary and grudging acceptance or whimsical or revolutionary defiance, the more important point that norms are mere constructed rules and not part of our "natures" is overshadowed—on the one hand by the conflict and the desire for conflict, and on the other by obeisance and security. Our greatest thinkers have distinguished themselves precisely in the manner of systematically questioning the heritage and justification of social norms, be they the norms of day-to-day behavior or those of scientific and philosophical discourses. These thinkers have recognized that society, even modern society, has other deeper foundations. Speaking of Gadamer's centenary birthday speech, his biographer noted:

> Everyone familiar with Gadamer recognized in his words his admonitions about the overbearing character of rules and methods in our society that tend to limit the freedom and judgement of the individual, founded on experience, tradition, and *sensus communis*. The unending ovations underscored the younger generation's

receptiveness to this message and their gratitude to Gadamer for being its foremost representative in the modern world (Grondin 2003:332)

Perhaps the hallmarks of any thinker of merit is that he or she does not stop at breaking the rules and braving the consequences but rather questions both rule and consequence and provides a history of how and why such boundary and transgression alike can occur in this or that social context. The thinker is prudent in social policy and in social commentary that lends itself to action only because he is a realist, and not because he is a loyalist. But in thought alone, ideally there are no parochial limits. Prudery in thought becomes only the enforcer of habit. Even a wider nonmoral caution must be cast aside for there to be full freedom of thought.

Not only rules and methods of the rationalized society impinge on thinking through the confusion of prudishness and prudence. We are at risk from the constant barrage of the marketing of commodities and their calculated manipulation of desire and sometimes even real need:

> Paid product endorsements, especially by real or purported experts, constitute a steady rainfall of deception. They betray contempt for the intelligence of their customers. They introduce an insidious corruption of popular attitudes about scientific objectivity. Today there are even commercials in which real scientists, some of considerable distinction, shill for corporations. They teach that scientists too will lie for money. As Tom Paine warned, inuring us to lies lays the groundwork for many other evils. (Sagan 1996:208)

Given that one of the functions of policy is to avoid reflection that may cost both time and money (simply apply this or that set of rules when encountering corresponding life situations) it should not be surprising to us that we become quite habituated to following direction. The content of these directions runs the gamut from buying a product advertised, voting for a political candidate similarly marketed, to more profound events such as marrying by a certain age no matter the prospects of intimacy and authenticity, training oneself for a lucrative career no matter one's personal interests, and abandoning one's place of birth for material or status gain. Most service industry managers are aware of having to memorize large tracts of policy manuals that attempt to cover every possible situation, real or imagined, that their workers might encounter on any given day. Rationalization, the odd outcome of the confluence of prudence and prudishness, produces a script to direct the theater of living. The division of labor has certainly extemporized the original sense that certain persons of certain ages are able to do certain different tasks. Yet today we compel ourselves to do within a very little range the same kinds of tasks over and over again. The factoring out of humanity from these activity areas and arenas is the ultimate point of policy manuals.

Prudishness in this context exhibits the fear of the unpredictable and thus the uncertain. Task efficiency is seen as the true expression of knowledge, even of truth. Prudence then provides the cover for what is prudish fear, by announcing the "one best way," in terms of time, money, and effort. We are often cautioned to proceed as if the worst could happen, to take the most conservative estimate as being close to reality, and in any event, the one that, whatever outcome, will disappoint us the least. This is "prudent," given what we know and what we cannot know for now. Both caution and fear are intertwined, and their tepid duet sounds also in fields apparently much more profound than those of the market and the service sector. There are also discursive scripts for the appreciation of art, music, and the doing of philosophy and science. Speaking of their dual origins in habit and anxiety—the one affirming what has been done, the one finding threatening what could be done—Gadamer suggests some implications:

> Basically both of these follow the same wrong path, but in opposite directions. One undervalues the old, while the other looks down on the new and the latest thing as aberrations. In either case, one actually spoils the view of what one believes one is favoring. In reality, we have the one only with the other: It is within the horizon of our experiences with the modern that the great art of the past becomes the challenging topic, and vice-versa. Here—as everywhere—one must see things together. This holds above all in the case of theoretical understanding. (Gadamer 2001:66)

The famous quarrel between the ancients and the moderns repeats itself writ small with each successive generation, though the contents of these repetitions have much more to do with the prevailing winds of moral and political fashion than philosophy or art, although popular versions thereof also have their place in this filial confrontation. For instance, in academics it is common to hear both those who disdain modern scientific knowledge—humanists, theologians, and scholars possessed by Plato and Aristotle amongst others—as well as those who abhor anything written before the enlightenment (say, about 1730 or so). These latter would be nominally my allies, given my own training. Yet while it is well to note that classical thinkers, as Sagan intoned, were able to question the evolution of the cosmos but could not or would not question the structures of their own societies, we must in this case do what Gadamer suggests. The "confrontation with tradition" includes both dialogue and dialectic. We must question what has come down to us, especially if it has the character of dogma, while at the same time learning what we can from it. For every misunderstanding of the empirical world to be found in, for example, Aristotle—and there are a great

Prudence and Prudishness

many examples of this—there is also a pithy bit of wisdom regarding ethics, politics, or interpretation of meaning. For every ridiculous line of smug self-aggrandizement in the Platonic dialogues featuring Socrates, there is a subtle piece of logic, social critique, or comment on the aesthetic realm. A consistent duet of learning and critiquing helps us to avoid the excesses of the other combination driven by anxiety and blind loyalty, that of prudence and prudishness. We need not be concerned that by doing so, we would inevitably become "conservative" or, irrelevant and old-fashioned. Even Nietzsche, who is generally thought of as one of the most radical thinkers of all time, had great, though not uncritical, admiration for the tradition, and often used his version of it to chastise the present day, especially when it came to the aims of education and the values of contemporary morality and rationalization:

> To where should they flee, if antiquity authoritatively rejects them! Must they not fall as sacrifices to those powers of the present, who day by day call to them from the tirelessly ringing organ of the press: "We are culture! We are education! We are the heights! We are the peak of the pyramid! We are the goal of world history!"—when they have the seductive promises, when precisely the most shameful signs of non-culture, the plebeian publicity of the so-called "interests of culture" in the journal and the newspaper, are extolled to them as the foundation of a wholly new, highest of all, ripest form of education! (Nietzsche 2004:73 [1872])

It is of the essence of all things fashionable to proclaim their superiority over things of the past. The "culture wars" in the United States have much the same timbre to them, given that the rearguard also embellishes the position of its attackers far beyond those latters' capabilities. Most importantly, both sides misrecognize how much they share of one another, in much the same way that science and religion often find themselves arraigned against one another, staring across a mostly imaginary discursive fence. We need to be more aware that one of the primary reasons that the new asserts itself against what is said to be outdated in our kind of economic system is that the new must sell itself as against what has been. In the words of advertisers, that which is to be sold and hopes to supplant what has been in place before it must be "new and improved." This basic imperative that pushes all brands and commodities into the public eye—not for their reflective consideration, mind you, but for their immediate consumption—is first formally critiqued in Nietzsche. It was one of the great ironic tragedies of the history of thought that a strange and perverse version of his work was mobilized by the Nazis some fifty years afterward to attack the art, science, and ethics of our own day. This fact should point up the danger of not using the dual scalpel of dialogue and dialectic in our dealings with history. Santayana, the philosopher who is oft partially quoted regarding his sense that to forget history was to inevitably repeat it had in fact more to say on the subject than this. Indeed, he reminds us that even if we do recall history to ourselves, we may *still* repeat it. This may be sobering to us, but we cannot be naive on this score. It very much depends on precisely *how* we remember history, and what we take from it—we cannot live it again, as it were, and we cannot know "the whole story" as if it were our own—that will circumscribe our successful living on in the present beneath both its light and shadow. No wonder then, when faced with the loss of mortal memory of what has taken place—whether in our own biographies or on the scale of grand world-altering events—that we shy away with the mixture of prudishness and prudence. We must be cautious, we maintain, in the face of not being able to repeat identically the past. Yet we also once again use this prudent value, rational in the context of partial memory, as a cover for the other part of ourselves that is tempted to

Prudence and Prudishness

cower beneath the folds of fashion in order to avoid coming to grips with our mistaken interpretations, and worse, our calculated ignorance of what our culture has already in fact been through, time and again. Thus we are guilty of both a guilt and an innocence. That we cannot know the whole story is not our fault. The vicissitudes of history and memory being what they are for mortal folks like ourselves provide empirical and reasonable bulwarks against transparent and honest knowing. This is our innocence regarding history. But we place ourselves in a false relationship to it if we either seek to cover it up, as if we had committed a past crime and no one is to know of it, or manipulate it for our own present day convenience, as did the Nazis. Yet further, we may ignore it altogether or pretend it has nothing to say to us because we are better and we have overcome the need for history itself. The "end of history" delusion follows this path. These constitute our guilts. This odd combination of "guilty innocence"—different from "innocent guilt" where one commits an act of which one is capable but of which one is unknowing—prevaricates itself especially with regard to what has gone before us, either in our own lives or within history in general. Prudence appears when we recognize the innocent ingredient of this recipe, and prudishness comes to the fore when we attempt to hide our knowing guilt. Nietzsche suggests that this potent amalgam can give us the sense that we are free from the inertia of history, from our own mistaken relationship with it, and from our own personal errors of living:

> You must understand the secret language that this guilty innocent uses before himself: then you would also learn to understand the inner essence of that independence that likes to be worn externally for show. None of the noble well-equipped youths remained distant from that restless tiresome confounding, enervating educational necessity: for that time, in which he is apparently the single free man

in a clerks' and servants' reality, he pays for that grandiose illusion of freedom through ever-renewing torments and doubts. (Nietzsche 2004:111 [1872])

That segment of society that most often finds itself laboring in the service sector today is not palpably different to these regards. What youth can be within these domains is an open question, given that one is at once training for something better while experiencing the world as something worse. And this schism holds only for the minority. It is still the majority of young people who do not attain higher education credentials and whose future is limited thereby. For most, then, the "illusion of freedom" is held together by the conflation of prudence and prudishness. The one says "I must conserve all I can in the face of a worse reality than even I experience today," and the other then demands "I cannot change the way I am for risk of becoming something worse." Our modern institutions either socialize us toward servitude of others, and thus point to freedom as self-serving and the ability to escape the other, or at once a servitude to self that is driven to disregard much of our own potential as dross and an impediment to freedom. Even the acts directed toward another may fall under this spell:

> Modern philosophical jargon has found a revealing term for this phenomenon, one of the many modern substitutes for love: "altruism." This love is not directed at a previously discovered positive value, nor does any such value flash up in the act of loving: there is nothing but the urge to turn away from oneself and to lose oneself in other people's business. (Scheler 2003:64 [1912])

Given that to know oneself necessitates a journey with and through the other, the idea of turning to the other is in principle sound. Without the sense that one must return, at length perhaps, to what one is oneself, this "walking in another's shoes" becomes vicarious at best. Many parents

Prudence and Prudishness

are guilty of this kind of altruism if they raise their children in the hopes that the latter will become some lost part of their own lives. The parent who discovers a talent that they also once had may be tempted to do this, or yet further, the parent who was not quite good enough at this or that vocation may manufacture this in their child with the hopes of a second life. Even genius is not aloof to this problem as we are told that Beethoven attempted to make his nephew into a virtuoso, when in fact the latter had little musical talent. Yet this relationship is only the most patently obvious version of nonreciprocal altruism born of the conflation of caution and moral anxiety. We often are tempted to make our spouses or lovers into that which we ourselves lack, to better service our perceived needs. This inclination may of course work both ways. We say that "one deserves the other" to this regard. Our superiors at work may foist this charade on us, or we may expect our friends to serve our illusory freedom from ourselves in some similar manner. All of these examples are merely at the level of the face to face, and their motives, though having wider patterns, may appear as idiosyncratic.

What occurs when entire institutions or policies become directed at remaking the other in an image that oneself feels saddled with and resents? One recent attempt at "taking care" of the other motivated by both prudence and prudishness is the appearance of certain kinds of sex education classes in schools. Social research notoriously documents that where there is present the so-called "abstinence education" there is in fact a *rise* in youthful pregnancies, sexually transmitted diseases, and, we may surmise, hurt feelings of various kinds. Yet we as adults would find the notion of educating younger people to the dangers of intimacy an ethical necessity. Not only given our own experience, where previous generations were at least officially held in relative ignorance regarding sexuality and thus left to their own devices to muddle through, but due to our present understanding that sexual matters are one of the crucibles of both beauty and its negation. The passions associated with erotism are only made more vulnerable through their adoration as a market fetish, where sexual youth is held up as the ideal human form. The formula of love in our day does not include the actual and authenticating feelings of union and loss that inevitably make their way back into the human equation in social reality. We are inevitably disappointed that what we had experienced does not live up to the formula as advertised. Whether virginal moments or long-term marriages, we end up looking for what did not occur instead of trying to understand our actions and motivations from within, and in light of the true other to self. In telling young people to conserve themselves, emotionally and physically, we are at once creating in them an awareness that could be taken as neurotic—in that one is told there is great danger and such is somehow unavoidable and necessarily "comes with the territory"—and mystifying a common human experience— thus making it all the more attractive in its taboo quality. This is a potent mixing of messages, although they serve the prudish/prudence amalgam well. "Don't do it" can only fail as a policy where "it" must define itself as a mystery and a transgression. Adult boundaries are present in our lives mainly through personal experience. That is, we do not continue to break the normative rules simply because we have often broken them before. The consequences we faced were enough, for most of us, to adjust our behaviors. We are also aware, though, that when enough of us break the same norms, the rules change. In setting up new rules for youth, we are at once urging them to be broken, as no human being can become mature without the experience of challenging what passes for authority or the tradition. Would it not be more mature on our parts to provide an authoritative and realistic account of human intimacy rather than demanding certain behaviors and formula from others?

I think there are yet darker motives in our attempts to force or even ask some one else to conform to specific rules regarding passion and intimacy. It is common that adults romanticize their own youthful experiences, whether or not these include diverse sexuality. We also have made a forlorn cult of the idea of "lost youth." Such nostalgia apparently keeps us going well into life until it implodes in the apparent mid-life crisis, which, with the extension of the quantity of life for some in the West, is gradually occurring later and later. There is no doubt much resentment and jealousy that older persons feel toward the young on the score of both aesthetics and erotism. We do not envy the young in terms of our now completed professionalization or finding a job, home, or partner, or facing the rigors of child-raising or the shock of either the sudden or gradual realization that one's bodies are finite and deteriorating. But just in this specific area that we have circumscribed for the young, where passion, beauty, and desire convene, we are at a loss. Where did *these* elements go in our own lives? Even if they continue, somewhat muted perhaps, we are made painfully aware by media and younger persons themselves that we are no longer the ideal, either to be loved or to love ourselves. The joys and novelty of the other to self, his or her physical form and the sensuality of their flesh against ours, is often unavailable to us as we age. It takes a creative ethics to distinguish between habit and heart here. The divorce rate—a social fact that has many antecedent variables—is often held up as a singular symbol of our desire for difference, or as an effect of those wishing to recapture times gone by. That we are aware of the questionable ethics of cheating on spouses, of breaking apart families with children, and even of pretending to love our mate while desiring someone else, only fuels the intensity of what can become resentment against youth. Abstinence education and all forms of intimacy education that stray from the objective probabilities and statistics of risk betray this jealousy and resentment. If we can no longer enjoy part of what is integral to human life, then our children will not be allowed to be more human than us. We will make them as we are, prematurely.

As petty as this may seem, there is a parallel with the notion of betrayal discussed above. Love betrayed can turn quickly to its opposite. Desire, passion, erotism, and love are in common contiguity in our society, and our ability to engage and indulge in the arts and intrigues of these human characteristics is gradually, and sometimes suddenly, betrayed as we age, gracefully or no. It is not surprising then to find that any of us project what is really resentment against the aging process as well as the processes of experience versus novelty and "innocence" against the physical likenesses of our past selves, our children. There is also a kind of freedom at stake, very different from the illusory freedom attached to those younger than us still making their way into society, as well as those yet younger who are still making their way into becoming social and fully human. This freedom, associated with the ability to experience the new in all things, and not merely those erotic, is often only noticed after it has been lost. It is an authentic freedom, because it participates in the hermeneutic circle that shatters previous prejudice and provides experience anew. We do not ever truly lose this ability in principle but we are often sequestered from it as we grow older, have more institutional and familial responsibilities, and may become cloistered in our logistical and financial abilities to travel and see other worlds. Indeed, part of the meaning of the phrase "where there is life, there is hope" includes this sense of freedom. We tend in fact to reproduce, as far as we can, this kind of freedom in our private lives. The private spaces of the home and hearth mimic both in space and time the boundaries that aging in society puts up at large around us. To cross the threshold of the private in our personal lives means for many to egress from the "unfree" space of public life:

> The public/private distinction, and the wide areas of negative freedom, is the equivalent zone in these societies to the festivals of reversal in their predecessors. It is here, on our own, among friends and family, or in voluntary associations, that we can "drop out", throw off our coded roles, think and feel with our whole being, and find various forms of community. Without this zone, life in modern society would be unliveable. (Taylor 2007:52)

Of course, we do not entirely cast off the dross of public personae in these spaces. Roles are played out here as well, and they are just as real and elemental in the portions they claim of our "whole being" as those portrayed in the wider public spaces. Nevertheless, Taylor has hit upon something that is important to us as natives in our modern society: We must have the ability to retire from the glare of our own publicity. Each of us is akin to a celebrity, though writ small, and privacy for North Americans is especially valuable in this light. The zones we believe to be more private, where we appear to have more power and control over who gets access to them and ourselves within them, are crucial to our sense that a self can survive the pressures of being a member of that very society that forms it. Indeed, we cling to this paradoxical relation of self and society, where the one is shaped by the other and yet can be transformed in turn. No doubt social forces and institutions are almost always more powerful than individuals, but it is well known how these latter sometimes find themselves in the crucible of immense social changes, riding the wave of revolutions, or simply having a bright idea when the time is ripe or even "before its time." We believe that we, in fact, can do this because there is a place where we can be apart from the rest, whether it be society at large or even, from time to time, all other human beings, including intimates. What the self is, at present, attains its selfhood through a combination of the naive belief that there is something more to ourselves than the sum of social roles, and the energy we expend in making that belief a reality.

Yet if singular vocation and care of the self is not universally available—one must have in fact time and space away from responsibilities to others, and many of us cannot escape the increasingly burdensome weight of family, job, health, and financial insecurities—there remains the panoply of artificial and ironically mass populace–oriented forms of escape. The entertainment commodities with which we are presented for mass consumption at first must pretend that they are directed to us as individuals, and that they say something personal to us. We may believe that "each takes what he can" from these messages and markets, but there is no real evidence for this. Indignation at the discovery that "my song" or "my movie" is also that of several million others I think is feigned at best. We are not so naive and sentimental to have ever truly believed that any act of an other person, especially one that is marketed to a public or has an audience of any size, could ever have been an act of intimacy, no matter how sincere its rendition. Public criticism of this form of attempted freedom and return to the self from being otherwise is also not likely to free us from the need to authentically construct some other space which is ours alone. The artificial space of entertainment that claims our hearts is the lighter corollary to the space of the polis which claims to represent our intellects. In fact,

> An increased diet of political moralizing and dutiful editorializing will scarcely liberate our presently impoverished political fantasy. Nor are we likely to liberate it by increasing the time allotted to [entertainment]. Nevertheless, I have the feeling that if the media encouraged, and if its audience could permit itself, more genuine escape, "away from it all", we would become

> stronger psychically and more ready to undertake an awakening of political imagination and commitment. (Riesman 1950:232)

We may be long out of the age when such an option for media is deemed plausible, but given that, as we shall soon discuss, criticism is itself subject to commodification, one can be entertained and piqued at the same time, by the same thing.

It is prudent to assume that the self concept can survive its public montage only by remaking itself as a kind of fantasy. The contents of that imaginary space, however, bear the hallmarks of prudishness and its transgression. That privacy is shot through with the erotic and the stigmatized alike means that we begin to consider ourselves deviant if we wish to carve out a space of intimacy of any kind. In this way, perhaps above all others, what merits pragmatic caution (being consumed by the public realm as one consumes a product) and what is tainted by moral anxiety (that all things that cannot be spoken or exhibited in that public realm are dangerous) prudence and prudishness mistakenly become as one. Thoughts are still free, it is said. But what if the sources that conjure thinking itself are not within our personal control? What if, after decades of formal education, primary socialization, on-the-job training, compromised relationships and marriage, and politics as compromise, there is nothing left to think about?

Bravery and Bravado

LONG BEFORE I was married, I was involved in a relationship with another remarkable woman. It was the kind of relationship shot through with an intense erotism and physical intimacy. Early on in our intimacy she confided in me that she had been abused as a child, though the scope and nature of the abuse remained mute for the time being. I recall acknowledging this in the most humane way possible, but in by no means in a satisfactory manner, as the helplessness and sobering demeanor that such news brings forth is akin to a kind of stultified awe. Our friendship was such that we spent many long days making love, and it was during one of these times that I seemed to experience a true displacement of consciousness. At the time, I was naive to the phenomenon and its supposed sources, and when I experienced it, or more exactly, when she and I experienced this together, I was again awestruck, though at an entirely other level than when she told me about her abuse. Altered temporality is a hallmark of passionate intimacy. Time seems to stand still, as one forgets the actual time. Beyond this, one often imagines feeling or undergoing a kind of union with the other, as if aspects of one's emotions had been doubled, merged, or traded for the other's. Neither of these effects of deep desire and connection was strange to me, although they had never occurred with such intensity and longevity until this particular woman came into my life. Yet what happened to me this specific time was well beyond any of these more recognizable manifestations of human communion. We were both fully mature adults, in our thirties, and though she had a body that appeared younger, neither of us could ever be mistaken for a child. I introduce this strange circumstance in this way because, after I had left the bedroom after a long period of intimacy and was returning, I was frozen in the door frame, my mouth agape. My jaw, as they say, hit the floor with my shock and amazement. For lying on the bed, complete with sweet angelic visage and tousled girlish hair, was what appeared to me to be the physical form of a six-year-old child.

I know I closed my eyes but the vision did not immediately diffuse or transform itself when I had reopened them. Only slowly, it seemed, did I regain the view appropriate to adult eroticism, the woman recognizable to me as my friend and lover. I stood blinking into the room, fumbling for some explanatory words that would reassure her that I was okay, and in fact this never occurred. It was she who spoke. What she said only heightened the disorientation, although her voice was her own, so to speak. She simply asked, "Did you see it?" In this context, one would wonder how to respond to such a deadpan query? I could say nothing other than, "What do you mean?"

"Did you see me, younger, much younger?" she asked.

"Yes, as a child, a little girl."

The conversation then began in earnest. It was striking that she had seen my reaction and had spoken first, with some concern in her manner and voice, but more so, that she already seemed to know what I had seen! How was this possible? It was then, holding each other both tenderly, but on my part, I dare say, a little tentatively, that she told me of her full experience as a young infant and child. A more grotesque series of events I have not yet encountered, nor do I hope to do so, and it would serve little purpose in recounting them here. Suffice to say that the abuse began as early as six months, and stopped, never to be repeated, at the age of six years. I was at a loss, disconcerting as these accounts always are. I said, "What can I do for you? Anything at all..." — my heart was open, as lovers always believe themselves to be.

"You have already done what no one has," she replied. "You have joined me where I was most at risk, where I was most hurt in my life. I have nothing but thanks and admiration for you."

Well, this was all very well, but as a staunch rationalist, more so at that time than I am perhaps today, this was hardly a real explanation of the event at hand. At best, I saw it as a *post hoc* interpretation, offering plausibility to the implausible.

"How did you know what I saw?" I asked.

"It could only be that, given your look of awe and anxiety. But I also knew that I felt I was regressing, I was seeing myself at that age during the time you left the room and returned. I was feeling what I felt then. Our experiences together, our love, has reopened all of this and made it as real as can be. Now you have joined me in this reality."

A past become present, represented by acts of powerful emotion in the present—that was what she was asking me to believe occurred. Again, this was still not an explanation, but a set of feelings and perceptions. Her senses were transformed and a vision appeared, as if in a dream. All of this was acceptable and even flattering. Yet I, too, had shared the vision, and far less flattering, needless to say, were some uncomfortable doubts I had about myself for many years afterward. Yet I did not truly think I had conjured such a vision because I had occult designs and desire concerning children, or saw her at length like a child and desired her for this. I was still mystified. I was only comforted by the fact that the shared moments of this vision had given her a kind of deeply satisfied joy, and, for a time at least, fostered an ever greater intimacy between us. I recall this event vividly. It has lost none of its other-worldly character for me, and I cannot imagine how it must have affected her, given that she claimed to be the impetus for it, and it was her youthful experiences that were its source. During those moments, what love could accomplish seemed to move beyond its mortal character.

Yet, in the sobering intervention of many years, I wonder what it really did accomplish. I no longer know the provenance nor life details of this woman. I moved on to a life I love and desired and trained for. Yet I still admit to some strange longing—and perhaps stranger, resentment, concerning the whole affair. The wonder and puzzlement about it appears in my life as something from a time out of time, from something that was beyond history in its ability to represence itself, much akin to a shadow of what she had claimed was the original "represencing". In stating the case to my professional friend, however—and one always tries assiduously to avoid playing the patient to friends who are at work all day with less fortunate versions of our own humanity—he found it immediately recognizable, and in fact, with much the same matter-of-factness this woman exhibited upon seeing my original reaction, declared myself to have had an episode of what psychologists call "shared perception".

"What is that?" was my obvious retort. A rare but known quality in the history of psychological thought, as well as in the experiences of clinicians, especially those dealing with forensic cases where there has been either an abuser—most often also at one time a victim of abuse—or someone who had been abused but who did not repeat the infamy, shared perception occurs when the person undergoing therapy has a kind of regressive flashback to specific moments when trauma had occurred in their lives, often in childhood. There are certain more or less formal means of accessing these kinds of events in another's consciousness, some of which are scientifically employed in therapy, although others are often more widely cited in parapsychological literature as "regressive therapies," including dubious claims concerning past lives and altered states of being. Beyond therapy, however, such instances can be experienced when the trauma matches up with current intense emotions, almost as if one were replaying the old events, or recreating the spaces in which they took place.

Again perhaps dubiously, I witnessed in my three-year sociological field study of disciplinary sadists and masochists that this was a strong in-group element of their theater; something that they urgently desired to take place. There was an impassioned eroticism about such spaces and their actors, whatever one might think of their form of "therapy."

None of this was directly relevant to my experience, my clinical friend maintained, but it does give one some perspective. What I had known was rare but not idiosyncratic. It was intense but not beyond the human condition. Most importantly, he reassured me, it came out of the most beautiful of circumstances and noblest of motives, spontaneously and without calculation—at least on my part, he interjected—and was not the result of a present pathology.

The implications of the theory of shared perception, he continued, are most radically that consciousness is liquid. It can be shared in moments of intense intimacy with another human being, whether that is conjured by erotism, strategic therapy, or even violence. Memory carries with it more than the mind's eye. Our very beings, or at least our perception of them can be "physically" transformed, and these transformations are in principle shareable across the once wide gulf inhabited by other minds. He then spoke of occasions when he had experienced shared perceptions, although they were far more disconcerting as he was helping dangerous criminals relive their trauma and come to grips with what he referred to as a form of *psychosis*. Literally, the fragmentation of the psyche, or self or even soul, "psychosis" has come to casually mean a kind of insanity from which there is no ultimate relief. This is not entirely correct, although we live with and must nurture our traumatized selves throughout our life courses—my former lover had a photo of herself at age four or so near her bed (not the same space as in which the event described above transpired) and referred to it as a kind of inner child who must always be cared for and loved. Rather, psychosis is a general term for the division of our sense of singularity, our naive sense that the self is only one thing and that we can really "know ourselves" as a specific reality and consciousness. This is, in fact, not the case, especially in our modern world, where the diversity of roles and scripts we must adhere to ultimately sabotage any sense that "one of us" is more real than the next. Of course, psychologists use the term to refer to extreme cases where one can no longer rationally manage the diversity of often conflicting roles and role-playing that our society requires of us. If we are forced into adult roles too soon—and what more extreme manner of this could there be than providing sexual pleasure to someone ten or twenty times our age?— our nascent sense of self becomes fractured along radically incompatible lines, perhaps never to fully recover. All of this I knew before I related the anecdote to my present friend. I never was able, due to the personal nature of my experience and my emotions, to put the two of them together. Now that it was done for me, I remain philosophically impressed, I think, more with the implications for the future of human consciousness as a whole than with the specific case and my part in it. Yet I also remain enthralled with it at a deeply personal level, as if I had shared some brighter version or vision of a trauma that I was fortunate enough never to undergo myself, or anything remotely like it.

My psychological friend went on to add two more things of note. One, that I had an experience that created a special bond with another person, and she with me, and that we were forever linked, no matter the distance, in a rare manner. And second, he recommended strongly against finding myself in these kinds of situations again unless I was being paid well for it! I definitely concur, though perhaps somewhat sardonically, with the second. Part of me still hopes the first to be true.

There was yet one more thing in my concernful friend's professional wisdom. He stated that above all, it took tremendous courage and trust for that person to share consciousness with me, and great nobility and courage on my part to accept her in a caring manner and to not reject her. Perhaps he was being generous in his analysis of my case. Yet it is this particular use of courage, of bravery, that I wish to explore in much greater detail. It is perhaps obvious that one example of true courage is that shown by all those who have suffered and yet continue to live on. This woman—and perhaps most humans—are heroes in this regard. One of the essences of the human condition requires an authentic bravery, and that is to simply live on toward death and gradually become aware of our own finitude. This is a challenge for those with the most kind and gentle beginnings in life, let alone those prematurely co-opted by a history of evil. That we can know true courage, what I am going to call here *bravery* and yet find occasion to confuse it with artificial, unnecessary, or sham courage, herewith called *bravado*, is part of the set of present-day conflations that endangers our sense of humanity and its future.

Taylor suggests one possible reason this confusion has come about. The shift in metaphysics from the theocentric worldview to the homo-centric one, where we become as humans the evaluators of our own worth, and we neither require nor even desire a judge other than ourselves, gives us both a sense of exhilaration and confidence, but also lends itself to abuse and *hubris,* false or arrogant pride:

> Above all, there is a certain pride, and sense of one's own worth; which is the stronger, the more acutely one is aware of what an achievement this is, of the unreasoning fears from which one has freed oneself. Part of the self-consciousness of modern anthropocentrism is this sense of achievement, of having won through to this invulnerability out of an earlier state of captivity in an enchanted world. In this sense, modern self-consciousness has a historical dimension, even for those—who are, alas, many today—who know next to nothing about history. They know that certain things are "modern," that other practices are "backward," that this idea is positively "mediaeval," and that other one is "progressive." The sense of historical placement can accommodate itself to a bare skeletal minimum of fact. (Taylor 2007:301)

There is a naivety about this new sense of freedom in that disenchantment also means that certain other creative freedoms of the human imagination are suppressed. The child-like ability to wonder at the world and to think thoughts anew, temporarily aloof from "the facts" of a Gradgrind, is more ably lost, as we saw above, with a rationalized world. This new world, with its new freedoms in attendance, is still not wholly free in that the entirety of what is human consciousness is not admitted to it, or is seen as quite deviant and even pathological, as we have just seen. I would not want to live in any other time and few other places than I do, and the sense of what is "mediaeval" to me certainly makes me wince, or at least roll my eyes. Yet history does not admit to radical and permanent separations with such casual ease. What we were we often are still, just as in our own personal lives we find it maddeningly frustrating to cast off apparent dross from previous versions of ourselves. The history of the human condition is such that the hand it places on the living is never quite dead, and that the living must undertake to bury the dead themselves as well as what is now dead within ourselves. The contents of these somewhat gothic categories may not be in fact very large, even though they often seem to us to be quite burdensome.

Two of the most bitter examples are the history of warfare from the early agrarian period to our own and the resurgence of forms of slavery around the world. Our rational, ethical selves always state that we wish to overcome such things, but at the same time there are people who benefit from their existence. The question, first baldly posed to the sciences by American sociologist Robert Merton—"Who benefits?"—immediately overcomes it's at first cynical glance by digging out the true sources for the continuation of what, also on the surface, seem like callous and even evil practices. We like to think that abusers hurt themselves also when they abuse, but it is just as likely that their own apparent lack of conscience—something "dead" within them, we surmise—prompts a different perception of what constitutes pleasure and what is one's "just desserts."

Although we have taken large steps in leaving the metaphysics of the previous world—the transcendentally oriented great chain of being that includes forms of consciousness divinely good and immortally evil born in agrarianism—there is little doubt that the moral inertia of its tenure in the human mind of ten thousand years or so rests heavily upon us still. What we *know* to be the case today often accords ill with our desires, or what we would *wish* to be the case:

> We are alone in the universe, and this is frightening: but it can also be exhilarating. There is a certain joy in solitude, particularly for the buffered identity. The thrill

at being alone is part sense of freedom, part the intense poignancy of this fragile moment, the "dies" (day) that you must "carpere" (seize). All meaning is here, in this small speck. (ibid:367)

What Taylor means is that we have lost our omniscient alter egos, and perhaps have thought to replace them with "altar egos." It is highly likely that this galaxy alone is teeming with intelligent life, so that sense of being in solitude is at best romantic and at worst egotistical. Bravery dictates that we seek ourselves through the other, putting all that we know at risk. Bravado is what finds a home in the apparent solitude of the present human condition. The same is true for the somewhat artificial boundaries within which we continue to group ourselves on earth. Nations and regions pretend to bravery in their imagined solitude. From the post-war period and into the post-cold war period, North Americans have nurtured the odd tandem of smug self-assurance and anxious paranoia. The one because we have been apparently the goal toward which many other nations gear themselves, the other because we are at least dimly aware that our world position has been had in part on their backs. Immediate post-war sentiments still bear an uncanny resemblance to our present situation, though now immanently passing before our eyes: "Both nationally and internationally, we are like a child who when young found other-direction quite successful (since he was always surrounded by a peer group) but who as an adult finds himself suddenly alone with the others looking up to him. The position is frighteningly lonely and conspicuous." (Riesman 1950:263) Bravado says in the face of this "What of it?", which goes along well with the kind of thinking we discussed at the very beginning of this book, which had always said to us that *we are the best* and thus it is quite natural that all others look to us for various forms of leadership. Of course this situation is rapidly changing from one fantasy to another in which we will be the center of attention. The lighter side to what many might fear is that this will give us the opportunity to become more reflective and more modest in our ambitions and perhaps to create a more humane society.

The combination, then, of the apparent official loss of a God defining metaphysics, along with the measurable loss in world influence, as well as the imagined cosmic aloneness of the human species as a whole, have permitted the dual manifestation of the loss of nature, and hence the anxiety surrounding our stewardship of the planet. The loss of "nature" occurs in two ways. The obvious one, that associated with bravado, is the conquest of wilderness and natural resources through technology and population expansion. This mock courage appears when we imagine that the biosphere will always recover from its wounds, and can be further bent to serve our needs and our needs alone. No doubt this fable is catching up with us daily. The "Club of Rome" report of 1972 famously gave us seventy years from that point to right ourselves with nature or be vanquished in a global catastrophe both economic and ecological. The less obvious loss of nature is the conquest of the concept of nature by that of culture. We cannot truly have ever been a part of nature once we ascended to the level of humanity, replete with language, tools, and the social contract. This, of course, is the origin of the paradoxical expression, "human nature," where seemingly universal traits ascribed to mankind are regressed into the primordial soup of biology. Social science has long been opposed to this kind of thinking (more on that in the final chapter). Yet all cultures have reinvented nature to circumscribe their influence in the world. Categories of culture are superimposed on those of nature, making the latter cultural. Plant and animal classification, as well as abstract forces that can be felt or observed as non-sentient often follow patterns of tribal or band kinship. Metaphor and metonymy abound here, and such categories—"folk classifications," as the anthropologists sometimes call them—are hardly scientific in the modern sense. Yet they are equally and obviously just as cultural as are the more recent systems of the sciences, and thus it is difficult to argue that "nature," as denoting a nonhuman realm devoid of meaning and anonymous to ourselves has really existed at all during the tenure of humanity. This is the bravery side of the loss of nature, as it was lost with the origins of what was human and afforded our earliest ancestors with the first opportunity to truly feel the kinds of risky exhilarations that Taylor speaks of as coming perhaps only in our own time. Surely this is not case. The lone hunter standing in his naked humanity, confronting the abyss of meaningfulness that is nature in the raw, torn from most of his primate instincts through gradual evolutionary trends, is of course a dated and sexist fable. But groups of hominids, with very short life spans and day-to-day subsistence, raising themselves above their cowering predecessors to stand within the new languages of religion, kinship, myth, and narrative is a story worth retelling until our own graves appear before us. This is the elemental crucible of human existence, and though some of us have become quite insulated in our prosthetic godhead from the effects of the day-to-day cycle of "nature" itself, we are nevertheless mature in our awareness when we take into account the presence of mortality within the very stock of vitality. No human escapes this fundamental bond, and it is perhaps the nadir of the necessity for the social contract in the first place:

> One of the sayings of the Greek physician Alkmaion runs: "We human beings must die because we have not learnt to connect the end with the beginning again and this is something we can never accomplish." This is a genuinely disturbing observation for it tells us that it is not something in particular that we lack, but rather

everything. Only the vital animating force of nature is able to do this.... (Gadamer 1996:97)

So the dual loss of nature in fact has committed human life to its own finitude. Our courage walks on toward this, while our hubris pretends to overcome it.

The lack of nature, both physically and conceptually, in turn projects itself into another realm where there appears a duet of effects. Gadamer explains:

> We live, on the one hand, in an environment which has been increasingly transformed by science and which we scarcely dare to term "nature" anymore, and, on the other, in a society which has itself been wholly shaped by the scientific culture of modernity. Here we must learn to find our own way. Yet we are surrounded by innumerable rules and regulations which ultimately all point towards an ever increasing bureaucratization of life. How, in the face of all this, are we to sustain the courage to determine for ourselves the course of our own lives? (Gadamer 1996:104)

No doubt the centralization of the "directions for living" in the state and its bureaucratic apparatus has been occasioned significantly by the diversity of values and the conflict of interpretations that is the hall mark of our time. The Protestant Reformation, the cross-cultural enigma exposed by colonialism and now neocolonialism, and the rationalization of a cosmos now dominantly subject to rational thought make it appear necessary that there should be a "third party" to oversee our multitudinous differences. "No one is above the law," we are told, no matter the host of available exceptions. Yet these exceptions are not themselves based in the fact that different cultural values hold per se, but of those who can make the most of the social distribution of opportunity in capital and the market. Just as applied science proudly tells us that a hydroelectric project functions equally well in China as it does in the United States due to the universal language of mathematics and, hence, engineering of various types, economists tell us that the market system is similarly objective and generalizable across all cultural values and through different languages. Following the rules is not to be bound by yet another system of values, but is rather to overcome the disparity and conflict of all previous values. Rationalization projects its method of the rational in this form of bravado. The world now runs smoothly not only because of the rule of law that supposedly has objective standards regarding human life and dignity but due to the economic system that ties us together in a global market that by its very nature out-competes all other previous systems and modes of production. No other culture need apply its traditions, and we can wholly forsake our own.

This tandem of the loss of the two natures and the creation of a monoculture of regulation and rationalization is, of course, the effect of the mythology that pronounces these achievements to be beyond both culture and history. We are painfully aware of the weakness of this claim, given that, on the lighter side, local cultures do in fact apply their own traditions to markets in so far as they are allowed by dominant institutions, and on the darker side, some of our fellow humans organize and violently resist the global effort of capital and rationalization. The perverse social movements that can arise in the face of neocolonial dominance make us shudder. The Taliban are perhaps the best current case in point. Yet this style of saying *no* to modernity is neither inevitable nor necessary. There are examples of other major movements that resist and transform the forces of the West to suit local needs and to make them, in general, more humane for all of us. Liberation Theology is an excellent example of this style. The myth that both the modern nation-state and its regulations, coupled by the extension of the Cartesian *mathesis universalis* into and through other cultures and languages must uphold, is one of not only objectivity but also ethical superiority. In fact, these institutions are no less historical in their construction and attempt and no less local in their morality.

Instead, we should put aside the bravado of our institutions and attempt to understand exactly what the other wants of us and wants for themselves. There is no need to engulf the entire world of cultural plurality, what there is left of it, for our species to ascend to one of its projected destinies, to return to the stars from which all life descends. If we ever encounter other intelligent beings, they may well ask us, *did you need to become as one culture to come this far?* The great diversity of human language, religion, and culture hardly impinges on the much greater forces of science and its applications, capital and its wealth creating forces, and rational institutions and their procedures. Is it not enough that these modern spaces have engulfed so much already? In fact, it is a great waste of energy and resources that could be directed and humanizing the margins of Western society to project these forces into other cultures who may well know their own way about getting along, at least with themselves.

It may be considered a grotesque comparison, but Hitler's quasi-war objectives on the Eastern Front ultimately sabotaged the purely military objectives of conquering the Soviet Union and, thus, likely winning the war itself. Enslavement, genocide, and the erasing of physical traces of his "subhuman" opponents were in contradiction—in the expense of personnel and material—with combat victory. Similarly, it may be the case that to imperialize our procedures, rules, and morality on others may in the end defeat wider and more noble objectives of environmental adaptation, pure research and discovery in the sciences, and the exploration of the cosmos. None of Hitler's objectives, military or otherwise, can be regarded as courageous, but we are arguably in a better ethical position today. At least some of our motives and desires can be seen as fruitful for all humanity. Even so, they need not all be forced down the throat of the other. Let the other come to us if need be.

Gadamer was once asked about what it means to in fact be *an other,* to take the other to self and to our culture quite seriously and to learn from them, and we can all learn a great deal from his response:

> Only by not thinking one knows what one doesn't know. The Socratic profession of ignorance or "knowledge of ignorance" is the decisive thing—if it's actually meant and practiced. In opposition to the whole of Sophism, Socrates always maintained that knowledge of the just and the unjust, and, ultimately knowledge of the good could never be an object of a particular *techne*, that is, a particular kind of knowing that exhausts itself (unlike every other kind of knowing) in the knowledge of the rules according to which one produces something. (Gadamer 2004:40)

It is certainly necessary that each of us have the how-to knowledge that is directed at a particular thing or process. By enacting such a form of technical knowledge, we can achieve specific goals, not merely in the day to day, like the goal of healthy hygiene or avoiding a car accident, but more broadly, such as longer life or avoiding bankruptcy. Yet this kind of knowing, which can be finished when it accedes to the narrow goal that lies at the apex of a conjunction of ordered rules, cannot suffice when it comes to the more fundamental questions of the human condition. Are there specific, hard and fast rules for happiness, love, mourning, and loss, and for understanding the discourse of history and of the other? No doubt we have rituals and prescriptions for these things, and popular psychology abounds with books and talk shows purporting to sell you the ingredients of the good life—and politicians marketing the recipe for the good society—but I wonder about these kinds of directions. I am suspicious that they are so available because we wish to shy away from the more difficult feelings that living presents, and thus the dangerous questions that may arise from them. The quick remedy is an element of bravado. The patient and even trepidatious reflection on our lot in life and our place in the cosmos is a characteristic of bravery. To claim the answer to the startling otherness of life situations—say the death of a loved one or even the loss of what appeared to be a secure job—is to close off further reflection. The presence of some other mind or some other culture in the world cannot be real. One might rather say that one need not have to think further with the other, or about him. Once again, the premature closure of dialogue, something we imagine Socrates to be the archetypical opponent of, is tantamount to suggesting that human knowledge is only technical and consists only of having the right information at the right time. Similarly then, self-knowledge would be the application of the appropriate rules and rituals in the appropriate contexts—and the ability to do this and to predict when it must be done would constitute the whole of self-understanding. Machines can work like this. We humans, however, are fated for something quite different.

    Increasingly, the sources of bravado in this sense have become stentorian in our lives. Not just in North America but everywhere there is a commodification of mass popular culture that aims at selling brands—music, sundries, politics, lifestyles, resources and objects, images and text to name a few categories. Human beings are given the impression that to possess and use a certain set of tools and to have or live a suite of deportments or comportments will not only make one successful but also fully human. What was in evidence a half century ago was merely the tip of the iceberg in this regard:

> The contents of the mass media are now a sort of common denominator of American experience, feeling belief, and aspiration. They extend across the diversified material and social environment and, reaching lower into the age hierarchy, are received long before the age of consent, without explicit awareness. Contents of the mass media seep into our images of self, becoming that which is taken for granted, so imperceptibly and so surely that to modify them drastically, over a generation or two, would be to change profoundly modern man's experience and character. (Mills 1956:3354)

In the post-war period there have been such changes of character—some of them animating the collapsing of the various categories that are the subject of this book. The concept of what character is, is now meshed with what we would more precisely call characteristic. If one has all of the traits, in the same manner as if one knows all of the rules, then one has the completed "character." The "whole thing" can be defined in the same way that the whole of a rule-driven process is quite literally the sum of its parts. There is nothing beyond what can be individually taken apart and counted, weighed or measured in some other way. Durkheim's "mechanical solidarity" betrayed this form, but the fact that all members of these small-scale subsistence societies actually did know everything that was necessary for there to be a culture of *that* character made such a claim an honest one. Indeed, even in the collective effervescence of the rituals Durkheim somewhat romantically inclined there was evidence of a *gestalt* transcending the sum of mechanical elements. Perhaps there was nothing else that could be imagined as necessary for those humans, our ancestors and our most marginal contemporaries.

Our situation is, however, quite different once again. One of the major reasons commodities and their consumption have proven so powerful and viable over our recent history is that they do *not* satisfy any fundamental human need. They do not address the *gestalt* of our diverse society that is clearly more than the sum of its parts, just as human individuals cannot be cloned in their personalities. Consumption cannot inherently respond to the human condition in its ambiguity and its finitude. (It is impressive that advertisers *have* used the essential happenstance of living as a characteristic for marketing items that concern safety and health, like winter tires and vitamins, but like all other such items, these "work" to a specific purpose hardly existential in scope.) Because consumption cannot inherently respond to the human condition, we are ultimately dissatisfied with the idea that there remains part of ourselves that is unfulfilled. We are, in other words, disappointed that we can still be disappointed, after all of our consumption, rule learning and following, and predicting, planning and managing. In addition, advertising and commodification cannot afford to truly satisfy us, for then it would be out of the game. The artificial creation of needs other than those emanating from the bravery of attempting to face up to the challenges of human finitude, the other to self, and the internal dialogue of self-understanding, consecutively can replace themselves and continue to fuel consumption itself:

> But the craving remains. It is a craving for the satisfactions others seem to have, an *objectless craving*. The consumer today has most of his potential individuality trained out of him by his membership in the consumers' union. He is kept within his consumption limits not by goal-directed but by other-directed guidance, kept from splurging too much for fear of others' envy, and from consuming too little by fear of his own envy of the others. (Riesman 1950:80; italics in the original)

This kind of stance that we tend to inhabit before our desires is well known. Mass popular culture and commodity fetishism are perhaps the two most obvious versions of the addictive quality of engaging human desire with bravado. This stance allows us to say to ourselves, *I can overtake my own desire, and in this way overcome it. I then can repeat the method anytime I feel unfulfilled, which is often.* Once again, a rule-directed set or series of actions is assumed to culminate in the goal that had appeared afar. If the goal is fulfillment, happiness, or comfort and security in the moment, then consumption and bravado may indeed be the addict's cure. But if the same list of goals are seen from an existential stance, from the point of view of one's life over time, and one's own fragile humanity in living on toward death, such a method is doomed to failure. To confront the challenge of such goals with bravery, rather, is to acknowledge them as holistic human needs and not as things with which one can enter contractual relations, or things upon which one can place an exchange value.

We also cannot afford to view such desires entirely in a rational light. Perhaps the strongest reason why we often behave as addicts do when we find ourselves conjuring our human needs in a compulsive or even obsessively repetitive manner is that they do not have only rational sources, and thus no mere rationality can satisfy them—least of which, the technical rationalization of the market and of following rules. Reducing desire and human need to rationality is another form of bravado, just as is their reduction to consumer or fashion-driven behavior. The goals of happiness and fulfillment, comfort, security, health, community, and love hold also within them the margins of our existence. We become aware of their importance in times of their concrete absence. The common idea that "you only know what you had when you lose it" speaks to this sense that our alertness to what makes our lives fulfilling is distracted by the very presence of that which we most desire. Sagan uses a poignant personal example to make a more general point about our humanity:

> The last words I found myself saying to my father, at the moment of his death, were "Take care." Sometimes I dream that I'm talking to my parents, and suddenly—still immersed in the dreamwork—I'm seized by the overpowering realization that they didn't really die, that it's all been some kind of horrible mistake. Why, here they are alive and well, my father making wry jokes, my mother earnestly advising me to wear a muffler because the weather is chilly. When I wake up I go through an abbreviated process of mourning all over again. Plainly, there's something within me that's ready to believe in life after death. And it's not the least bit interested in whether or not there's any sober evidence for it. So I don't guffaw at the woman who visits her husband's grave and chats him up every now and then, maybe on the anniversary of his death. And if I have difficulties with the ontological status of who she's talking to, that's all right. That's not what this is about. This is about humans being human. (Sagan 1996:203)

Very few of us understand, or are even interested in, the mathematics and physics that were the threads of the great scientist's vocation. Yet all of us can immediately recognize the emotions and life events that made Sagan like ourselves, another human being searching for meaning in the world and in the universe. He reminds us, "We make our world significant by the courage of our questions and the depth of our answers." Bravery is to be found and lived through in the nonrational realms of human emotion, life, love, and death, as much as it can drive the rational adventure of modern knowledge in science and philosophy. In fact, it rather must do so, if we are to maintain any authentic link with what we are trying to understand.

Those scientists who question human conduct, mores, morals, and norms are just as human as ourselves. I sometimes have the odd student who is critical of what they take to be my personal feelings about my fellow humans and their sometimes laughable and pathetic, sometimes awful thoughts and deeds. But the true misanthrope makes a poor student of society. He has too much of an axe to grind, always seeking to expose what he feels are men and women at their worst, which he then takes to be indicative of their true colors. In actual fact, we humans occupy the entire spectrum of value and concern, and each of us, if we had been born into the "right time and place" are capable of all of the best and worst of human history, whether it be saving the lives of millions through scientific discovery or ethical social leadership, or yet murdering millions by running a concentration camp. Our specifically individuated contexts of socialization—where and when and how we grow up as we do—tend to limit our imagination (aside from the more massive institutional limits about which Riesman and others warn us). Yet it should not be such a task to imagine ourselves in others' shoes, walking the road to salvation or destruction, as the case may be. We as a species walk those twin roads together and perhaps never more so than today, given our technological capabilities for good or ill alike. The person who only sees the worst in others is likely to be more interested in bringing out only the worst in herself. Similarly, we cannot be optimistic to the point of giddy naivety. The person who claims an unabashed adoration for her fellow humans is also a poor social scientist. Both the misanthrope and the naif are missing about half of the equation. It is striking, and also perhaps sobering to the rigidly rational mind, that the great moral systems of human history had no trouble recognizing the dual inclinations of agrarian and post-agrarian human consciousness. As stated, the tree of knowledge does not allegorize knowledge for its own sake but human knowledge as precisely occupying the value spectrum from good to evil and back again. Science, when it fails to take into account not only the uses to which its discoveries are put but also the very humanity of those who practice research, will also miss the point of what makes its work not only relevant but sacred.

A striking example of a student of society who transgresses both extremes of naivety and misanthropy is found in Max Scheler's little book on "ressentiment." The malicious existential envy that inverts cultural values in the manner of the proverbial fox and the (now sour) grapes is signified by the French term for extreme resentment. In spite of both peering at the social world darkly and then naively wishing it to be something it is not, Scheler reveals some insights relevant to our discussion. It is always somewhat disconcerting when, in noting the value spectrum of human knowledge, science itself proceeds to take part in it just as partially. In the midst of such analyses we inevitably also find that the heady mixture of analysis and object that looking awry of a new perspective:

> A further rich source of *ressentiment* lies certain typical inter-family and intermarital relations. Above all there is the "mother-in-law," a tragic rather than ridiculous figure, especially the *son's* mother, in whose case matters are further complicated by the difference in sex. Her situation is one which the devil himself might have invented to test a hero. The child she loved since its birth and who loved her in return, the son for whom she has done everything, now turns to another woman who has done nothing for him and yet feels entitled to demand everything—and the mother is not only supposed to accept this event, but to welcome it, offer her congratulations, and receive the intruder with affection! It is truly no wonder that the songs, myths, and historical reminiscences of all nations represent the mother-in-law as an evil and insidious being. (Scheler 2003:39 [1912])

Anthropologists often report that one way of dealing with these tensions is the institution of the so-called "joking relationship" to prevent the other person from becoming a more genuine nemesis. Mother-in-law jokes are not uncommon even in our own modern society, and they speak to one of the more practical uses of bravado on the part of sons, wives, and in laws. Courage here is muted in the face of the needs of social relations. No doubt we have gotten beyond any reproductive or subsistence needs of that these older social organizations existed to fulfill. What we have not overcome is our need for intimacy and community of some kind, for to overcome such things as these would mean the transformation of humanity into something quite different. Indeed, spiteful resentment and envy are also the hallmarks of mitigating real social tensions with the pretense of bravado. The trading of slightly edgy insults, sometimes on the topics of one's sexual potency or impotency, trading on the idea that one's blood relations might in fact secretly desire one another, and that the in marrying relatives are actually usurpers to this role, yet further, that we in some Freudian manner seek out surrogates for our mothers or fathers in lieu of having sex with them are all well known topics. Some of these myths are ancient, and some of a recent variety, as when psychoanalysis enshrined some of this as a theory of intentionality. We have gotten so used to this by-play in our social relations that the jokes and sexual innuendos have themselves become subjects of other forms of humor. The sense that we owe our parents a debt that cannot really be repaid in any existential form is reflected in moralities that resonate in our version of the collective conscience. "Honor thy father and thy mother" is an edict that expresses such a series of debts, and imputes still others, especially if we do not heed it regularly. The possibility of bad conscience haunts all those who forget to service a debt, particularly those that cannot be fully paid off. Memory itself tends to urge us to counter with bravado, as if we can pay off the existential promissory note. The selectivity of human memory, moreover, often conjures a dangerous mélange of resentment and the inversion of debt. Who really owes whom here? Some parents are abusive, some negligent, some incompetent. All parent child relations are fraught with some tension, at least minor violence, and always some version of coercion, as unsocialized smaller humans-in-the-making come into their own by first coming into a society that is not their own but which appears to own them, at least for a time. Such a mix of memories that all of us carry around with us, akin to a contract in which both parties are indebted, is likely not to hail bravery as its accountant. Bravado suggests, rather, that debt can be assuaged and cast off without real loss to either borrower or lender. Hence the notion that, ultimately, neither of these have a viable social context in which to prevaricate their dual bondage. Atwood, in her pithy lecture series on the concept of debt, reminds us that "Without memory, there are no debts: a debt is something owing for a transaction that's taken place in the past, and if neither debtor nor creditor can remember it, the debt is effectively extinguished. 'Forgive and forget,' we say; and, in fact, we may not be able to forgive totally unless we forget." (Atwood 2008:75) The saying might be more realistically rendered in its inverse, forgetting coming first and only then forgiveness as a kind of abstract and liberating feeling. Of course, its takes guts to forget a slight with the foreknowledge that in doing so we will not only forgive it but also forgive ourselves for our apparent inaction. Much of our socialization, especially that of males, rebels against the idea of simply letting something go. All the more so, the idea of "turning the other cheek," offering up another part of our selves to the slings and arrows of outrageous fortune would make us sound like masochists. Part of this negotiation with an ethics is due to bravado, which tells us to fight back no matter the merit or value of the battle, and bravery, which adjusts the standard of what is worth fighting for. The first calls into play unreflective mass socialization that either supports or threatens the social order, and thus antedates the political or moral rationalization of norms. "Boys don't cry" or "stiff upper lip," depending on whether you were born in North America or Britain, dies hard. Yet being able to "pick one's battles" expresses a kind of courage that is harnessed when we judge it to be truly needed, petty injustices of the adult playground aside. It takes courage to face up to the fact that the structures that maintain social order often do so at the expense of freedom and thought, desire and justice alike. Our notion of the good society has more internal threats than those that emanate from exogamous quarters. In fact, we notoriously need the idea of the external enemy to shore up our trust and faith in our own internecine value conflicts and the institutions in which they remain unresolved. To blow the whistle on such organizations, whether of persons or of ideas, is to call into question the very sense of what we have taken for granted as just:

> To see this questioned is profoundly unsettling, threatening ultimately our ability to act. Which is why in earlier times we see people lashing out at such moments of threat, in scapegoating violence against "the enemy within," meeting the threat to our security by finessing that to our integrity, deflecting it onto the scapegoat. In earlier periods of Latin Christendom, Jews and witches were cast in this unenviable role. The evidence that we are still tempted to have recourse to similar mechanisms in our "enlightened" age is unsettling. But it would not be the first such paradox in history, if a doctrine of peaceful universalism were invoked to mobilize scapegoating violence. (Taylor 2007:456)

In any society, no matter its ideal doctrines, the very fact that we hold our own ideals as somehow sacred necessitates an inevitable comparison with the supposed ideals of others, as they manifest themselves in the world. If these others appear to be threatening we take action on two fronts. The external enemy must be vanquished, or at least silenced and made irrelevant. This is more convenient than the action on the second front, which is to cleanse our own community of those who hold or appear to hold values similar to the other whom we have just disdained. McCarthyism in the United States is an oft-cited example of modern scapegoating. The reaction to the Dixie Chicks, discussed in some detail in the first chapter, has a similar tenor. Ultimately, the nation-state is culpable, as it usually at the very least aids and abets, if not outright sponsors, such attempts at internal "cleansing." The modern state is seen to represent the polis that in previous times was made up of merely the local community. There is a direct road, however, from Salem to Nuremberg. In principle, no one is exempt from the charge of treason, and all of us must be cautious in the face of the potential power of censure and stigma that the state maintains as one of its weapons against its own citizenry. One of the reasons why there is always a potential charge of betrayal to ideals in modern society is that large nations contain many regions of consciousness, as we have already mentioned. The diversity of cultural and political norms allows blocks of citizens to organize along normatively ideal lines—whether or not these norms are actually lived out on the ground in any concrete manner—and thus confront the traitor *en masse*. Even a popular band with a large following found themselves the scapegoats by taking what turned out to be a courageous stand against what was at the time a largely popular conflict—generated originally by the mobilization of a contrived mechanical solidarity in the face of, what else, an external threat to our ideals emanating from an other who became an enemy—and yet already was evident to many non-Americans as unjust, overcompensatory, and based on false allegations. It is well to remember that *an other*, by definition, cannot truly "betray" us. The other *already* has a different view of things, and is no traitor in expressing this view. Perhaps we react with such vitriol due to our own doubts about ourselves and those immediately around us. We know we cannot rely on the other as a matter of principle, although our cultural ego may imagine that, because we have the best worldview, others should somehow immanently see it for what it is, and if they cannot immediately adopt it, at least pay it its respects and leave it alone. The Roman state set up a similar circumstance when they required noncitizens and believers in other religions than that of the state to ritually pay lip service to its gods, while turning a blind eye to alternative practices that did not threaten the polis. We can dare say that Christianity, taking over this role as state religion in the late fourth century, was not at all as tolerant. Suffice to say that our sense of what is sacred in these realms is another element of bravado, for it rests on the suspicion that our neighbor may be our enemy and that the out-group is "naturally" disposed to attack us in some way. Any combination of cowardice driven by paranoia shows itself by our reaction to it: inflated and egotistical claims to moral superiority and a lack of reflection on the responsibility we may have for a situation that reflects injustice and deteriorates into violence.

 I say, "turned out to be courageous" when referring to the Dixie Chicks' comments regarding then-President Bush when they were touring in England, because at first one could be forgiven if they saw the apparently unrehearsed statements emanating from the stage in the middle of a concert as an attempt to engender enthusiasm for the band itself from the largely anti-Bush British crowd. Indeed, in attempting to at first dissuade their American fan base from practicing scapegoating, the band members even used this theatrical "heat of the moment" sense as an excuse. It became obvious, however, as the band returned with integrity to their original position, and upon viewing documentary footage of the original event, that the comments were a sincere attempt to let the British fans know that not all Americans, even at the height of enthusiasm for the Iraq war, were unreflectively patriotic in their sentiments. Any time there is a person or group that stands up and says, *hey, wait a minute, we are not going along with this, and here's why*, there is the immanent possibility of the feeling of resentment and the corresponding action of a witch hunt. This error of bravado, the ability to contrive solidarity in the face of a perceived threat, brooks no resistance, especially at first. It takes time and usually also a series of events that suggest empirically and even personally that we were not quite right after all to set up a context where sober second thought is issued. Of course, resistance itself can be artificially contrived, and in our kind of political system this is indeed the kind of contretemps to which the citizen is often subject. To respond to the force and flow of the original solidarity with outspoken and seemingly individuated critique is, however, to not only place oneself at personal risk—during the subsequent tour of the United States in 2003 there was even a death threat against the lead singer of the Dixie Chicks—but is to call into question the ideals that we *thought* had been the sacred and thus morally right source of our feelings of distrust and enmity. Doing this second thing is tantamount to questioning our right to exist. It is not then surprising, in this light, to observe historically and in our own time that some people react against this by either suggesting that the questioner should actually die or by going out and actually killing them. The error of bravado then is compounded by an utter paranoia that regresses us into the shadowy "evolutionary" netherworld of "fight or flight." If we imagine we are in a position to enact the former, through strength of numbers, the alliance with the state or other countries, or even a personal and sometimes incautious egotism—"I don't back down to anyone"—then the questioner or critic had better take cover.

Politicians are always quick to jump on what appears to be a grassroots bandwagon, because they are continually paranoid about maintaining the good wishes of their electorate. They also have a sense that they in some way "represent" the interests of "the people," and thus when these interests change, the politician must change along with them. Yet we at the same time entrust the leader with superior insight—a *gestalt* of the diverse insights of the collective will of ourselves and our community, say, that cannot be expressed as one voice by the crowd itself—and surely this must include a reflective stance that does not immediately graft itself on to the most common opinion of the day. It is ironic, though by no means rare, when other figures of popular culture assume the role of political leadership by an uncalculating reflection on the current state of public opinion and call it into question. This is all very well, and we cannot but praise the bravery of whistle-blowing wherever it may take place, but ideally, those that we ourselves give the calculated task of representing the polis should ultimately be the ones to not merely reflect our opinions and needs but to be reflective upon them. We need to hear the *hey, wait a minute* from those we democratically set up to oversee our society. Such a system then would not be weakened in the face of fashion and corruption. None of us need be "fans" of politics to fully participate in it, and, unlike popular music groups, the polis and its system of governance would not win and lose market and following depending on its apparent popularity, although specific ideologies might. Bravado in this context could not survive a cautious and reflective diversity of views and the necessary coming to terms with the conflict of interpretations which *always* exists, no matter what power the fashion of the day may seem to have over us. Yes, such diversity is often frightened into silence, but this kind of success we should disdain. We rightly could, in our time, and especially when we compare our "progress" against the situations of our ancestors, feel ashamed at such a petty and fascist victory. As Gadamer suggests, "… people go wrong when they try to force [others] to conform to the systematic ideal of methodically constructed knowledge, a model that neither can nor should suffice for them." (Grondin 2003:268) We have already critiqued this kind of rule-following technical knowledge, but it is striking how quickly it can assume the role of thinking in periods of perceived crisis, as well as its almost omniscient presence and hold over us in the circumstances of mundane daily life. Bravado encourages us to see what is massively constructed as the rules for the many as in fact something we ourselves have invented for our own uses and by our own process of reflection. Given that the egotism of bravado cannot admit to itself that ultimately there are forces all around us that impinge on our freedom and our individuality, personal desires and even needs, society's rules and fashions, ideologies and state *autodiktat* are perceived as emanating from the self. At the very least, bravado must say to us *I can use this, it is good for me, even if it not originally be my own*. Nietzsche suggests that this attitude is characteristic of part of modern knowledge itself, and that philosophical thinking has, depending on the local context, either learned from popular lack of reflection, or that it has lent credence to it, or both:

> Knowledge, consumed for the greater part without hunger for it and even counter to one's needs, now no longer acts as an agent for transforming the outside world but remains concealed within a chaotic inner world which modern man describes with a curious pride as his uniquely characteristic "subjectivity." (Nietzsche 1983:78 [1874])

The drive for security and the desire to be insulated from the vicissitudes of living on may be one source of modern knowledge and its rationalized compartments. Perhaps more generally true, however, is the sheer immensity of the possibilities of knowing in our time. The uses to which knowledge is put often provide the false courage of bravado in our sense of potency and technical virtuosity. "We can solve any problem through technology," for instance, or "If we know all about a problem, we can fix it" are statements that the bravado of rationalization issues. "All" about a problem tends to be cunningly sly in its appearance, and technology appears to initiate as many problems as it apparently fixes. Whom do we ask when we need to know something, and is one expert more expert than the next? Who benefits from solving certain problems while allaying others? How do we know when enough is enough? Like the problem facing ethics in the world, the problem of authentic courage is one of facing and negotiating with the consistently unnerving inconsistency of the human condition. Not that this conundrum is imposed upon us from without, nor is it conjured without at least some of our assent or even active prevarication. Rather, what we identify as a problem with society is in place due to the conflict of interpretations surrounding what makes a good society and, further, what makes a good life.

Sometimes, as we have seen, it even can be sourced to what is said to be a human being and what is not. When it gets to this stage, anything is possible, up to and including genocide. Knowledge then becomes what one has to be now to be human in the eyes of what is now constituted as full humanity—an Aryan citizen of the greater Reich, for instance—but equally important, knowledge is also the means to liquidate the nonhuman. We can apply this extremity as a metaphor for the general human caution or yet compulsion to deny or attempt to eradicate the influence of the strangely alter to oneself or the exotic culture seemingly opposed to one's own community and society. Ultimately, in a society that is as large as it is diverse, where values and their interpretations sometimes radically differ amongst regions and subcultures, the idea of knowing anything at all in a certain and secure manner dissipates, and the desire for knowledge is either sabotaged by nihilism or ethnocentrism, or is pursued in the manner Nietzsche suggests, as a way to collect and enumerate the ephemerata of history and philosophy without a sense that its vital force remains viable only through the living dialogue from which this knowledge was originally born. The bravado of the rule-bound life, as paradoxical as this may seem, provides in fact the very space for false courage to preen. The peacock of bravado rests upon the assumption that most persons will accede to rationalized predictable circumstances, and thus extremes of rule-bound behavior—the sense that a highly rationalized society and a criminal state based in part on a false science could have a heroic destiny and a noble humanity as the "thousand year reich" is our most vivid recent example of this kind of bravado—can appear to be impressive and even courageous in the face of what has been the quotidean past. Once again, an extreme exemplification only serves to highlight the underbrush of the day to day regarding our taste for what in the end are mere magnifications of the mundane.

    The modern mass media is almost addicted to providing examples of our fellow humans' rude or deviant behavior, the more sensational the better, although almost all of this "deviance" is actually an application of widespread social norms in a manner not usually socially sanctioned, or at risk of some negative sanction from the state. The interest in "true crime" investigation series or even melodramas featuring criminal families attests to this interest in the vicarious voyeurism of bravado. And not merely are we voyeurs. We are also animated by the sense that fellow humans can, and do, live differently from us. We may be so with the express purpose of condemnation—many of the criminal investigation shows not only propagandize rational applied sciences such as forensics but also the morality of the legal code and the authority of the state, as represented by the technocratic minions of the "criminal sciences." But we also are fascinated by these fictions precisely because we do not really believe that these alternate lives and actions are possible, at least for us. They do not, in the end, respond in a fulfilling fashion to the questions surrounding the insecurity of modern human knowledge. They can only with bravado cleanse the world of momentary doubt, whether through forensic virtuosity or moral dictation.

The popularity of such series, movies, and novels is also linked to our sense that an authority or expert—whether person or system—can report and record the answer for us. We can quite literally desire to be told how to think and what to know, when thinking itself is neither trained for nor practiced and knowledge means only information:

> Such reports persist and proliferate because they sell. And they sell, I think, because there are so many of us who want so badly to be jolted out of our humdrum lives, to rekindle that sense of wonder we remember from our childhood, and also, for a few of the stories, to be able, really and truly, to believe—in Someone older, smarter, and wiser who is looking out for us. Faith is clearly not enough for many people. They crave hard evidence, scientific proof. They long for the scientific seal of approval, but are unwilling to put up with the rigorous standards of evidence that impart credibility to that seal. What a relief it would be: doubt reliably abolished! Then the irksome burden of looking after ourselves would be lifted. We're worried—and with good reason—about what it means for the human future if we have only ourselves to rely upon. (Sagan 1996:58)

We would become more than human if our contingent knowledge was transformed into certainty. Yet I wonder if we might indeed rather become less than human. Consider what it means to doubt. All forms of authentic courage could be said to flow from the mortality and ambiguity of the human condition. To have certain truth would be to abolish unpredictability. We would always know what we were about and where we were to be going. Rationalization, as we have seen, seeks to establish precisely this kind of regime. Follow the rules and you will gain a kind of freedom; freedom from doubt if not necessarily freedom from pessimism or freedom from the world as it is. Traditionally, putting ourselves in the hands of another form of being is mimicked by our modern reliance on a system of experts. Yet arguably the greatest expert on society of all time, Max Weber, strongly suggested that we not allow experts to run our affairs. Science, he stated in a famous address of 1918, was to be used to inform public and democratic decision-making. The broadest consensus was to be sought, and while problems could be handed over to a society of experts for deliberation and reportage, such a group was to have no further dealings with the work of the polis, other than participating in it as persons and citizens like the rest of us were to do.

The problem with this model was, of course, that the language of science was unequally distributed. It is perhaps all the more this way today. How can we be "in the know" when we don't in fact know anything about what the experts say to us knowledge is about? How is it possible that a general consensus be brought to the fore in the face of many and contradictory special interest groups, both within the larger society and within circles which partially succeed in excerpting themselves from society at large? On top of this, there remains the problem of too much of a certain kind of knowledge, the kind that through mere inertia rests ponderously on the shoulders of present-day humanity and that we have merely inherited, without much resistance, from our forebears. History as a dead weight upon the living can masquerade as deeper knowledge of the present if we strive only to reanimate it in the forms both of fetish, memorialization, and cynically making it do our convenient and contemporary political bidding. The stultification of potentially salutary social change is often the result:

> We know, indeed, what history can do when it gains a certain ascendancy, we know it only too well: it can cut off the strongest instincts of youth, its fire, defiance, unselfishness and love, at the roots, damp down the heat of its sense of justice, suppress or regress its desire to mature slowly with the counter-desire to be ready, useful, fruitful as quickly as possible, cast morbid doubt on its honesty and boldness of feeling; indeed, it can even deprive youth of its fairest privilege, of its power to implant in itself the belief in a great idea and then let it grow to an even greater one. (Nietzsche 1983:115 [1874])

The inertia of mere history as knowledge, rather than the dynamic of historical consciousness as the effective and working rewriting of the tradition in the face of the living present, acts only to assist bravado in its ongoing task of pretending to know in the face of doubt. We may wish to employ this charade in front of our children from time to time, to allay a sense that it is unfair to let the innocence of childhood breathe prematurely all of the vapors of mortification that such a world as ours often wafts before us. However, this theater rapidly turns to chicanery if we do not expose it in due course, like the commercial myths of Santa Claus and so forth, and perhaps even the capitalist myths of the work ethic and of equal opportunity amongst others. It is a delicate relation. In order to have precisely the kinds of abilities Nietzsche suggests are the flower of youth and of all youthfulness no matter our chronological age, we do need to be kept in the dark for a certain period of time. The numerous thresholds of enlightenment we set before our children are both manifold and uncertain in their order. When, exactly, do we expose this or that as a fraud, pious or otherwise? As with all things human, the demythology of what it means to live on in the social world is as vague in its presence and installments as is the contents of its demythologizing. Like the attempts to suppress sexual desire in youth through "abstinence education," bravado almost always imagines that it answers the question of doubt by being stentorian. The loudest voice proclaims the closest truth. Even if this not be so, the rhetoric of apparent strength gains followers, who, as Sagan noted, are longing to be led in some manner that suggests the eradication of doubt, most especially their own. It requires all of our courage to resist both destroying the incubation period of childhood so that it matriculates to a potentially heroic youthfulness without losing its sense of both curiosity and awe, while at the same time not making our temporary myths so fraudulent as to be dangerous to maturation itself. Given that these are very much the kind of decisions Weber had in mind when he warned us from placing them in the hands of only experts, or letting experts speak as somehow more than mere human beings themselves, we can perhaps now see more clearly the kind of fix we have gotten ourselves into over the course of the preceding century.

Yet the most uncomfortable truth human beings must face is not simply the power of the inertia of what has been. It is that our very sense of who we are masks the scope of this power. We can only stand against it by standing within it, understanding it by standing under it, as it were:

> In fact history does not belong to us; we belong to it. Long before we understand ourselves through the process of self-examination, we understand ourselves in a self-evident way in the family, society, and state in which we live. The focus of subjectivity is a distorting mirror. The self-awareness of the individual is only a flickering in the closed circuits of historical life. That is why the prejudices of the individual, far more than his judgements, constitute the historical reality of his being. (Gadamer 1988:276–77)

The inertia of history carries along within it a geometrically inclined dimension of inchoate human individuality. By this I mean that each of us is more the other than we are generally willing, or even able, to admit. The other, as long as this person is shaped by historical forces and social location similar enough to ourselves, is more akin to us than they are of their own sense of self. We tend to downplay this kind of connection not only due to the empirically evident distance between our physical forms in space—contrary to the case at the atomic and subatomic levels where there is no such empirically identifiable gap—but more importantly, due to a morality that individuates us in the eyes of the law and in the eyes of God. We are responsible for each other in the collective conscience because we are basically the same person and all acts are acts on behalf of a greater whole. Such a community is refracted by diverse historical forces, but it is not entirely muted by them. We have claimed the right to be different from one another by eschewing the original community of kindred aspects of a single soul, but we cannot get so far as claiming an egress from the general history that animates human life and gives it its unreflective form. It is only bravado to suggest that we are beyond history, or that history has come to an end. Bravery consists not of vain attempts to step outside of one's own history and the history of one's cultural fellows, increasingly globalized, but of painstakingly recollecting and dismantling the layers of socialized sediment that have built up both our souls and our selves through the birth of happenstance. This task is crucial to begin to distinguish ourselves not just from others we know or imagine, but ultimately, to begin to form a distinct version of selfhood that takes into account all which is not of my reflective self, that which stems not from examined thought but merely from acknowledgement and acceptance.

Socrates famously says in the *Apology* that "the unexamined life is not worth living, for a human being." This is so most profoundly for us moderns, because the unexamined life is not in fact our own life, it belongs to history in a manner unreflective and passive. That we, in reflecting upon our lot, still belong to history and always will do so, does not mean that history is impassive and unyielding. What Gadamer means by his phrase "the confrontation with tradition" is the dialectical aspect of the dialogue of which we are. Belonging to history in a reflective manner in fact changes history and creates what has been called "historicity." This technical term suggests both that we are born into history and borne on its currents but also that we rewrite the course of history by examining our position and construction within it. Human beings can and do alter the course of history all the time, most of us in small ways that affect only some of those around us. Yet even here, the process of the examined life is most important, as we generally imagine that we should make changes in the world that are positive and ethical no matter the scale. If we appear to be an uncaring and oblivious society it is mainly due, I think, to our lack of knowledge of the effects our way of life has around the world. We are always most concerned about ourselves, or guises of ourselves that we find the most recognizable. We cannot escape our own history, but we are not doomed to accept it as it has come down to us. Yes, our prejudices are necessary and as ritual and habits they become as if they were organized necessities. Yet the proof that mere history in this sense does not have an omniscient presence and hold over all that we do is offered by the act of thinking itself. Reflective thought is itself revolutionary to all histories.

The bravado of reflection lies in its comparison and observation with other forms of what remains unthought. We do, of course, require that the other allows him or her to be set up as a model for either rejection or emulation. We look to one another to see how we ourselves "measure up," and we do this in a multitude of ways. But this manner of reflecting is short-circuited by the desire to either be like the other or to outdo them, or to at the very least be inconspicuous enough to avoid incurring their disdain. We think for the others' sake in each of these guises of comparative reflection. We imagine, with bravado, that the process of thinking can either help us to overcome the dross of the other, or escape the other's social gaze, or achieve a universal acceptance. In none of these do we think with relation to our own historical situation. We are, as Riesman famously put it, "other-directed." That is, our ability to think is yet further defined, and thus maintained in this narrow definition, by what we think others are thinking, especially, of what others are thinking about ourselves. We sacrifice a good deal, including the ability to hone authentic and courageous self-reflection, in pursuit of the desire to be a part of the inertia of a general history not of our own making. In doing so, we support what has been the case without regard for what might yet be the case, bad or good. We *voluntarily* submit to the direction of only what made us human while detaching ourselves from the lifelong process of becoming humane:

> If the other-directed people should discover how much needless work they do, discover that their own thoughts and their own lives are quite as interesting as other people's, that, indeed, they no more assuage their loneliness in a crowd of peers than one can assuage one's thirst by drinking sea water, then we might expect them to become more attentive to their own feelings and aspirations. (Riesman 1950:373)

What makes one's own, our hopes and fears, is of course never entirely idiosyncratic, never entirely alone within society. This is a good thing, for sharing the dreams of what it means to become humane in the face of the merely human, and what it means to rewrite history in the face of how history has, up to this very moment, been written, requires that we share our thoughts with the other. This sharing is the dialogue of which we are. The risking of self in the face of the other is no risk if we only imagine the other to be like ourselves, or try desperately to make ourselves into a picture of the other. Rather, we must authentically, and with courage, risk what we know ourselves to have been in the face of the world as it is.

We are not, in fact, the same human beings the planet over. Although each of us may be capable of acting or even being, given the right place and time, the entire gamut of what humans have been over the course of our species history, we are in fact not placed in every possible social context, and thus we must use both our imagination and our critical faculties to explore the tapestry of humanity from specific historical vantage points. The other is a crucial, perhaps *the* crucial, element in this exploration. We truly become who we are through the journey as others to self: "The idea that men are created free and equal is both true and misleading: men are created different; they lose their social freedom and their individual autonomy in seeking to become like each other." (ibid:373)

If the entire scope of thought be limited to mimicry, whether of each other or of media models, then bravado will be the only option for the mimic. If we, however, engage with the other in history and with what we have been as other to ourselves in the present, bravery will no longer be a nemesis, but one with us.

Criticism and Critique

"EVERYONE'S A critic." How often we hear this plaintiff whenever there is resistance to the commentaries of others, whether or not they are objectively fair or just. And even here, as with many of the contexts we have already discussed, who are we to say this or that sense of things is the right one, the fair and the just? The conflation of engaging in criticism and engaging in critique is the result of both not knowing what is reasonable to expect from others, and feeling that these perhaps same others expect unreasonable things from oneself. At the same time, criticism lacks the historical consciousness, and also springs from sources generally judged to be negative, like *ressentiment* or *schadenfreude*, malicious existential envy and the taking of pleasure at another's suffering, respectively. Really, these two ethical concepts are two sides of the same critical coin. We certainly must travel far to encounter a fellow human who seems to be above these feelings in all quarters of his or her life. We also rarely meet someone—and perhaps rarely feel this way about ourselves—who seems aloof to the potential unfairness of others, or yet who asks only of others the absolute just, or of only that which they would have these others ask of them. Because we often find ourselves in situations where we are quite rationally sure we are being treated unjustly, and just as surely think that others of less merit than ourselves are getting all the breaks—the old ditty "rain falls on the just, and on the unjust fella. But more upon the just, 'cause the unjust stole the just's umbrella," speaks to this angst—we are very willing, often over rather petty matters, to engage in calling someone out under the guise of defending ourselves. That is why, at some time or other, everyone is indeed a critic.

Consider the following two (true) scenarios, one in which I am in the right by the usual normative standards operational in the contexts at hand, and one in which I am not:

    a)   A student who I have judged as a rather good one, active, bright and interested, with ethical motives and long service record to various communities, hands in a paper for my class which has all the earmarks of having been written for another class. The theme of the paper we had discussed in a very general manner in my course, but the content of the paper, the references, and the argument all seem to hail from a rather different quarter of the social sciences, indeed, a different discipline entirely. Yet I am astounded that this student, say, compared to many others, would do such a thing, which in the academy is considered to be cheating or plagiarism. You cannot copy yourself. If you hand in the same paper two different times without permission you are making it do "double duty" as it were; getting two grades for the price of one effort. Student culture aside—where at least for some, getting away with a good idea concerning cheating is seen as a good in itself—the professor, who is both a representative of institutional policies and much more importantly, the integrity of scholarly discourse, has the authority and the moral location to make a judgment in this kind of case. Indeed, we must make such a judgment to be fair to all the other students who do not appear to be bending the rules. Yet in order not to appear to be merely a rule-enforcer, and thereby avoiding the reflection needed for a truly ethical action, as we saw above, the professor must imagine possible contexts. In this case, my sense was that I should tell the student that this paper appears to be a very good one and yet off topic for this class. I want the student to get full rewards for such an effort, and so if there is another class in which they can hand it in, to feel free to do so. The demand I make of the student is, of course, that they write another paper for my class, more relevant and using the references we discussed in our class, and then hand that in. This response allows the student to save face in a context where they might stand to lose the respect of the professor, while as well not having to accuse the student of something that may in fact be the result of a total misunderstanding of the terms of the assignment (which in this case was hard for me to believe, but I had no real proof that it wasn't so). If indeed this was a case of plagiarism, the student would be let in on the fact that I appeared to know this to be the case—or at least be very suspicious of it—and yet have a way of saving themselves from the rather dire official consequences of academic dishonesty. Ultimately, of course, the student could stick with handing the paper in and suffer a much lower grade than would be comfortable. For a good student like this one, this trade-off— the low grade in one class versus the time saved by handing in a paper twice and perhaps getting a much higher grade in the other context—would almost certainly be untenable. In the end, the student took my advice.

b) A former female colleague and I almost never got along. We disagreed about most things academic, including pedagogy, the role of theory (she seemed to have no role for it), the concept of literacy (she seemed to have none), evaluation and the systemic process of tenure and promotion, and finally what the university was ideally for. She was a victim, I thought, of hyper-rationalizing, which had ironically made her irrational. For all of these "intellectual" reasons I felt I was justified in my dislike of her, and when I eventually moved on to another job I gave her no more thought. Recently my wife suggested that I had been too hard on her and for no rational reason. It was then that I finally realized what lay at the basis of my feelings against her. It was not her apparent lack of intellect and bureaucratic mindset that set me off. Rather, her looks, age, and bearing had reminded me of a former girlfriend toward whom I still had some strong enmity. I had had an emotional, not a rational, reaction to her, and the source of this was a spurious analogy between two very different persons. I had likely treated her unjustly from the very beginning of our acquaintance and now had no way of righting that injustice. I vowed to examine my feelings concerning the person from my intimate past, so that I would not project them on another from my collegial present.

It should be obvious that in scenario "a" I was in the right, and in "b" in the wrong. But aside from the particulars of each case, is there a contrasting principle that can be generalized from both of them into any circumstance? I believe there is, and it has to do with the contrast between criticism and critique. In the first situation I engaged in critique, the second, only criticism. What is the difference? Critique takes into account one's own possible biases. In this case, was I sure that I had communicated the assignment to my students transparently? Had there been moments where misunderstanding was possible, or even probable? How could I be sure that her paper was indeed directed at another class? Was my reading of it biased in some manner hitherto unthought? Critique also leaves open the door to an extension of the situation into unknown territory. I thought I knew exactly what I wanted from the assignment, what I wanted my students to accomplish. Were their means of accomplishing these goals that were different from what I had imagined? Were my students capable of originality beyond the rubrics of the course, or even their major? As well, critique suggests that the original goals may themselves be flawed or at least incomplete. Was there another way of thinking or communicating that addressed the problems of the course better or more deeply? Finally, critique emanates from a position that is authoritative and not merely any authority. I was the professor and scholar and pedagogue, and she the student. I could be more confident that I knew how to not only ask the questions and engage in the dialogue and dialectic that all authentic critique demands but that I could instill some of this in my students. In a nutshell, the concept of critique includes its own critique. It is transparent to itself and possesses no ulterior motives, or at least has the means to expose them through the dialectical process.

    In the other situation, however, I was actually being quite uncritical even though I imagined myself to be engaging in the same process. I was looking for things to criticize because I had not yet critically evaluated the sources of my own disposition. The emotional irrelevancy of my actions and thoughts had not been exposed, and indeed, could not be once I had locked myself into the process of criticism for the sake of criticism. The ability to be self-reflective, necessary in any human relation that aspires to a full humanity, was lost at the moment of contact, where I recognized at some semi-conscious level that my dislike was more important than anything that might follow from this then new relationship. No doubt this is how many of us treat certain other "categories" of being human. One bad experience leaves us closed to change and reappraisal. In scenario "b," I had closed off the possibility from the beginning of this colleague being in fact herself. I had taken from her the ability to be her own person, but also, more drastically, to live in the present and to be fully human. Criticism then is a process by which we rationalize motives with dubious relevance or none at all by providing an excuse to continue to nurture their presence. In this way, criticism is always unreflective and cannot lead to genuine insight about either ourselves or other people. We are fortunate when we have others at our side that can see through this, and who are not blinded by what seemed to only us to be "objective" reasons for our behaviors. This necessary otherness, akin to all of the characteristics of the other already discussed, is the place of incipient critique, rather than mere criticism. It should be obvious that we cannot always get to this place on our own, especially if we have undergone some kind of trauma, sometimes petty, in previous situations which seem to be alike. Indeed, it may be that those with obsessions of some kind may be compulsively engaging in automatic criticism to protect themselves from too painful a self-reflection. Criticism has become habitual and routine, akin to an aspect of one's primary socialization. We need not think to engage in criticism, but here, in its extreme forms, we cannot think at all.

    The conflation between these two concepts merits some patient dissection. It seems clear to us that criticism is not only easier to accomplish and that it occurs more often in the day to day, but that it brings some satisfaction, *schadenfreude* perhaps, that makes it a little addictive. The fulfillment of engaging in critique seems to be of a more esoteric and philosophical species, not the kind of thing we normally want to practice day in and day out. It is likely that most of us have been in situations that are potentially socially awkward, like first dates, or yet further the first physical intimacies with a new friend. How often we find relief when one and one's partner finds something that we both dislike in other people. We might be at dinner and could engage in smirking about others' clothing or their conversations. We might be attempting to celebrate intimacy, but unsure that we have "performed" not only correctly but *well*, and thus we engage in laughing about past lovers' inadequacies. For most of us, such a list of circumstances is likely to be a lengthy one. But what of the list of contexts where we have actively reflected on our own lacks, whether it be of mere taste or of authenticity in love?

The main problem with criticism is that it is not what it appears to be. Not only does it rationalize ulterior motives, as we have said, it justifies the idea that we can have such motives and not feel that we have to expose them to others. Criticism engages a new take on ethics, one in which we extend the normative notions of what may be left unsaid, thereby also extending the space of our own private doings at the expense of others. Further to this, and perhaps paradoxically, criticizing others is also an attempt, often surreptitious at first, to bring them into conformity with how we think the world should work and look. What I see in others is what I choose not to see in myself. What I imagine I want to see in others is what I imagine myself to already be. There are enough of us engaging in this kind of misrecognizance of both ourselves and others that it takes on a form of general social control. Like rule following, here we are attempting to re-create the situations where people conform to our imagined ideals, or remind them that such ideals exist and that they are currently straying from them, and at their own risk. We are all potential "rule enforcers," as Becker stated above, and aside from gossip, criticism in our sense is a primary vehicle for controlling the social scene.

Not only individuals practice criticism for this goal. Mostly, persons in face-to-face situations don't even realize they are doing this, and have some other set of what are thought to be more personal motives, as I did when I imagined in scenario "b" to be maintaining intellectual standards or even rising above the general rationalization of the mind that can occur in large organizations, even those dedicated to improving it. However, general social control is also taking place. We semiconsciously and "voluntaristically" aid larger social structures in maintaining social order by engaging in criticism without reflection. We instill the expectations of "the rules" in others even when we imagine ourselves to be transcending those rules. Taylor suggests that large-scale historical social reform aimed at reorganizing the ways in which persons think about their social life and how they interact within it have important common features: They are active and interventionist, they attempt uniformity amongst a populace through homogenization, and they are rationalizing in very much the sense we have discussed above (cf. Taylor 2007:86). I want to point out that the same processes are at hand in much more personal and individuated spaces of social action. Whenever we give into unreflective action of this sort, criticizing others' for their very being perhaps, our attempts at making them conform to some other manner of being themselves take on the guise of generalities. This is so because we do not know much about the one we are directed against. Writ large, this same process occurs in warfare, where "the enemy" is hardly human at all, or if so, an insult to the better humanity that we alone, or with our allies, represent. We know little about them, but criticism never needs to know, as it already imagines that through making a sardonic comment, or by becoming the executioner, it has all of the relevant knowledge at its disposal.

Obviously, and perhaps equally so, we ourselves are not at all immune from the criticism of others. Perhaps we have strayed from the social norms—even, unfortunately, by reflection and the practice of critique, say—and must be brought back into line by the tenor of the society at large, or its institutions. "Getting along" is of the utmost importance, and given the conflict between persons and cultures in the world today, to be indicted as being "part of the problem" seems a serious charge indeed. We engage large-scale social institutions in the fight against not only authentic critique, but too malicious forms of "uncritique," like criticism in certain social contexts that seems to most others to be out of line. We also must try to manage our own cultural biases in an increasingly diverse social world:

> The mass media today are expected to perform ten-minute miracles of social introductions between people from a variety of ways of life and background. The entertainment fields serve the audience less and less as an escape from daily life, more and more as a continuous sugar-coated lecture on how to get along with the "others." (Riesman 1950:160)

Whether in visual or print media, the general message of popular culture is that the norms of the day—set up by no one in particular, and signifying no apparently specific ideals nor further suggesting an ethics—are to be upheld by becoming a member of someone else's "generalized other," a sociological term invented by American social philosopher George Herbert Mead to designate the inchoate and nonempirical idea we have of society at large. This society is not made up of real persons, mind you, but simply other people whom we imagine to have internalized their free and voluntaristic support of the social fabric as it appears to be woven through all of us. What we are able to further is a kind of continuity of criticism directed at those who would disturb society at its best, the criminal, the psychotic, the deviant, who either through hyperbolically observing some of our social ideals—self-centeredness and greed or even altruism and charity depending on the context—or through inattention to the most basic of social needs—the addict or the libertine, perhaps—tear up the warp and weft of the tapestry of sociality. We have no doubt become much more subtle and complex in our scripting of the loyalty to mundane sociality and its attention to criticism. The plots of many television melodramas today require sustained attentiveness that often corresponds to the shelf life of the program itself, but the moral of the story remains the same. Similarly, serialized mass market fiction may disturb us, but only because the characters in the story do not do what we imagine they are supposed to do. They make us uncomfortable, as do the villains and sometimes even the heroes of television, because they fail to submit to the flow of our own criticism, or that their criticism is misdirected and misguided: "The reader is not encouraged to make great demands on life or on himself. Rather, [it is assumed] that there is a solution that involves neither risk nor hardship but only the commodities—interpersonal effort and tolerance—that the other-directed person has in surplus stock anyway." (ibid:164).

Riesman mentions soon after that fantasy and science fiction were at the time the only realistic portrayals of a more whole humanity. The striking use of allegory in these genres mimics that of ancient and Shakespearean literature. It may well be exactly the same situation in media today, where the scripts and plots of popular science fiction sagas like *Star Trek* often seem to take the viewer a little ways beyond the casual and predictable affirmation of social norms as they are imagined to be. These kinds of contrivances may be on the way to critique, because they push the consumer to engage in real reflection about *how* one lives, and why one feels one must do so in this or that manner. This stance is quite different than merely understanding oneself to be juxtaposed with another as a kind of object or even as an altered version of oneself:

> Reflection, as the capacity to take up a certain distance towards oneself, is not the same as a relation of opposition towards an object. Reflection is rather brought into play in such a way that it accompanies the lived performance of a task. This is our real freedom, which enables choices and decisions to be made even as we participate in the performance of life itself. (Gadamer 1996:53)

The distanciation of critique calls one out of one's willing and often unreflective action in the world of others, and calls the world into question as merely a world of altered selves. The radicality of otherness is presented to oneself in a new way, and we open the door to experiencing the world as a living and thoroughly diverse undertaking. "Performing one's life," of course, can also mean that we merely play out socially scripted role behaviors, but it can also mean that we play these roles consciously and reflectively, and at least pause, from time to time, to imagine how we might do things differently, and how others might be if they would step into the "role" of the reflective practitioner of living.

Given that the stimuli from media and other institutions of socialization to critique and reflect are seemingly so few in number, it is impressive how many people nevertheless try to engage just those faculties of consciousness. It is perhaps too much to say that our mass society has no opportunity for rational and systemic critique. It may be that even critique can be commoditized, with "great ideas" sold to the highest intellectual bidders, and indeed, the university often seems like the marketplace for such transactions. Yet authentic critique often can begin not in some philosophical ivory tower but in the very guttural and emotional quality of feeling the tension and anxiety of one's everyday life. Perhaps this is the space from which the most stringent critiques in fact emanate. A classic example of the link between mundane frustration and incipient social critique occurs in Mills' description of retail sales, hardly dissimilar to our present version of the service industry in all of its guises:

> Salesgirls often attempt identification with customers but often are frustrated. One must say "attempt" identification because: (1) Most customers are strangers, so that contact is brief. (2) Class differences are frequently accentuated by the sharp and depressing contrast between home and store, customer, or commodity. "You work among lovely things which you can't afford to buy, you see prosperous, comfortable people who can buy it. When you go home with your low pay you do not feel genteel or anything but humiliated. You either half starve on your own or go home to mama, as I do, to be supported." (3) Being "at their service," "waiting on them," is not conducive to easy and gratifying identification. (Mills 1956:174)

I very much doubt that the construction workers who build the home they can never live in, the wait staff who do not eat the gourmet food served, or perhaps can only afford to eat the fast food that they serve elsewhere, the mechanic who works on the machines they will never own or drive, or yet the teacher who is charged with preparing the youngster for an academic or professional career replete with degrees that far outranks her own feels much differently from the retail staff at a million consumer locations. Yet frustration at the unfairness of the contrasts that are part of capitalism as we know it today is not enough to engage in critique, although it can point us in that direction. As well, critique of this Marxian sort is but one of the vectors of living the reflective life and avoiding the disingenuousness or mere criticism.

We may well be aware of the disjunction that permeates the material relations of society, what Marx and Engels called "alienated consciousness" born for them in the different relations to the means of production. From Riesman to Taylor, there is a strong current in post-war social critique that suggests we more or less simply turn ourselves away from the spaces of these tensions into alternate lives and worlds made more real through enhanced technology in the service of entertainment. Some of the sacrifices people may imagine having to do with the less devout bonds of community and fidelity, loyalty and trustworthiness, but that is probably an artifact of historical reportage, where the farther one recedes on the horizon of that which is chronologically and sometimes materially past, the more likely one is to encounter only records of the elite strata of society, and thus have little enough idea how most people lived, let alone what they thought about. Acknowledging this is usually accomplished by focusing the sometimes contrary lenses of either nostalgia or criticism on the recent past. The *Leave it to Beaver* era of the post-war baby boom is a favorite, though in actual fact diffuse, target:

> In a way, the costs may be hidden by the fact that we are especially indignant, even today, about some of the restrictions and oppressions of the 50s: women confined to the home, children being forced into moulds in school. We feel these things should never occur again. Whereas the costs, like the unravelling of social connections in the ghettos, or the way so many of us "channel-surf" through life, come across either as bearable, or perhaps simply

"systemic," and thus to be borne regardless. (Taylor 2007:480)

There is both nostalgia and criticism here, and in an odd way, they open one door to a more radical and authentic critique of both these shallow and politically convenient other elements. When criticism is of the *auld lang syne* sort, it tends to link social variables that are either disparate and unrelated, or related only indirectly, in the service of at least the intimations that *maybe things were better off before* this or that social change occurred. At the same time, this intimation remains at the level of a subtext, because we cannot truly prove that such and such changed this or that but only that we have observed the presence of one thing and the absence or transformation of the next. Not unlike Hume's notion of scientific causality, the "constant conjunction of events," social scientists and social philosophers often rely on more of a personal sense that aside from the overwhelming and inchoate observation that the world has changed, much more importantly than the specific contents of such changes, is that the world is no longer the one that *I* knew, the one I grew up and into. Older people notoriously feel saddened and alienated by this, and younger people, mostly unwittingly, may be seen to exploit it and enjoy their elders' premature passing on. This simple feeling of being divorced from what one took as one's wider home, the world as we have known it, accrues to it the new and disconcerting feeling of being a guest, with our presence being regarded as sometimes unwelcome and even annoying, in a new home made by and for others. The world becomes as we *had* known it, and we cannot fully know the new world in the same way.

This shift produces a number of new rhetorical strategies to cope with or to rationalize it. The most stringent of these attempts to actually either reverse the clock, pushing back to the world as was known (sometimes seen as "conservative"), or in its "progressive" version, attempts to push yet further to a more just future, of which the new world is seen as merely a partial form. Diplomatic incarnations of both of these kinds of criticisms obviously exist, where those to be converted to the argument, whatever its historical inclinations, are cajoled into agreement by a more passive and seemingly more reflective stance that does not directly speak to the problem or the source of the tensions involved:

> You might think that before they denounce unwelcome research findings, major corporations would devote their considerable resources to checking out the safety of the products they propose to manufacture. And if they missed something, if independent scientists suggest a hazard, why would the companies protest? Would they rather kill people than lose profits? If, in an uncertain world, an error must be made, shouldn't it be biased toward protecting customers and the public? And, incidentally, what do these cases say about the ability of the free enterprise system to police itself? Aren't these instances where at least some government intrusion is in the public interest? (Sagan 1996:217)

Are we kidding ourselves here? How many rhetorical naiveties can be mustered in the pretense that we are surprised or even at all skeptical of how such a system actually works? Why would large and powerful interest groups be interested in interests other than their own? Do governments even represent persons in a more ethical manner than do some corporations? And just what is the "public interest," anyway? In capital, we are well aware that profits before people rules the day.

But it is not quite as simple as even that. Some people do benefit immensely from profit-making activities, though relatively few. Even the most reflective and outspoken critic of the "bourgeois mode of production" stated baldly that it was by far the most liberating form of stratified society in history, mainly due to increased chances of social mobility, which were nil in previous forms of social organization and subsistence such as agrarian societies. On top of this, because everything can be bought and sold in capitalism, everyone's talent is potentially a commodity and thus is potentially valuable, though in practice, once again, Marx realized that there was quite a narrow strip of talent that was actually of interest at any one time. This "alienation from human potential," or from our "species-being," was of utmost importance to his theory of consciousness and to his understanding of the relations of production. Thus for real critique, the social situation at once appears complex and divergent. We must compare our woes not only with the general human suffering but with the burdens of history, without regard to whether or not those burdens may be said to have been ideologically overcome. Some profits, for example, come from real boons to the human condition, though we may question whether anything that is of value to all as humans should ever have a price on it and thus be inevitably socially distributed in an unequal manner. Whether as profound as cancer treatments, or as mundane—but much more universal—as toilet paper, such inventions ideally would be part of our common lot, not subject to the market or its elite interests.

Ultimately, our notion of intelligence is bought and sold, and often constructed to undertake duties related to either profit or the maintenance of rationalized institutions that protect those who accumulate wealth and oft-times exploit those who in fact produce it. Our notion of authority in general is permeated with the combination that criticism should be directed at the apparent margins of capital but also at the scions of wealth and power. Both those who pretend to authority through institutional status, and as well those who have authoritative positions because of their own experience and knowledge through living and thinking are subjected to unreflective criticism sometimes rhetorically masked as feigned naivety:

> This situation is [in] evidence precisely at the level of intelligence which finds it difficult to submit to medical authority. Whether in the form of insight or of a blind lack of insight, reflection here does not involve the free turning of attention towards oneself. Rather it remains permanently under the pressure of suffering, of the will to life, of the fixation on work, profession, prestige, or whatever. (Gadamer 1996:55)

The fact that we are most often directed by the duress of either social life or of human life itself is not necessarily fatal to thought, but it does impress upon us another obligation to thinking, that of taking into account our true motives. To ask myself, "What exactly am I doing, or desiring, in this situation?" is the kind of question that lends itself to regress. With each response, with each layer of consciousness that is peeled away and which thus exposes another, I can ask the same question, and then without even coming to complete certainty, respond yet again with "Is this really the case?" This is another reason why critique, as opposed to criticism, can appear so difficult to us. Whatever the topic investigated— and we can demand of others that they aid us in this quest, practicing a home-grown version of the methods used by social researchers; interview, dialogue, interpretation, for example—it is no doubt much more convenient to take stock only so far, to step around the shadows of motive that may lay beneath the surface of action. This is not to say that our intents are hidden away in some alternate language of the unconscious, to be revealed only by the dialogue of dreaming, say, or some waking *faux pas*. The life of the mind is not limited to only anxiety or desire. Taking stock in a conscious way is the accounting of thought, not the metaphor of what had been unthought. That transparency in human relations is a kind of comfortable myth we tell ourselves is not merely a convenient fact to keep social scientists (and psychotherapists) employed, though it also performs this function: "Of course nothing in human life is ever really self-evident; where it so appears it is because perceptions have been narrowed by cultural conditioning." (Riesman 1950:11) Yet at the same time we cannot step outside of ourselves in some meta-cultural manner. All of what we learn, including what we learn to think with, is a matter of such conditioning, and thus it very much matters what kind of socialization we are subject to as to whether or not we are narrowed beyond the point of reflection and self-critique or whether the cultural vista presented to us opens up onto both farther and more intimate horizons.

Even if we often feel that we are being forced to do something that (or be someone who) is not part of who we think we are or whom we would rather be, most of this pressure comes not from a patently and suddenly exogamous source. We have internalized our cultural conditioning and made it part of us. We had submitted to it as youngsters, but we now are ourselves part of its reaffirmation and maintenance in the wider world. We even proselytize it globally, though most of us passively do so through our consumptive practices. So it is not that we are ranged over against some other set of forces, other to the self. What we ourselves are is also the home of both unthought and criticism. This is why criticism is most often directed against others, rather than at ourselves. When we are self-critical, we often find that we are feigning critique in order to accomplish some other end. The false-modesty of the suitor is well known, for example. One's own status may be derogated temporarily, or within certain contexts, in order to win the affections of a desired other. She might say in her head about me "Well, he is so down to earth after all, a man of the people and not always thinking in the stratosphere." Self-deprecation usually has an ulterior motive. We are well aware that our lives and strengths are fragile enough, and our desires and desperations struggle against such impermanence with all their human minions. Yet even feigned critique can be a passage to the real thing. If you consider how I might conspire to make myself look other than I actually am, or at least, usually am, such a process requires some reflective thought. This thinking may not go far enough, as it has been hijacked by some other passion or intent than self-understanding for its own sake, but its activity reveals the ability to parse, plan, and undertake a reflective process. It also exposes further the point regarding social conditioning. Even with vulgar or local intent, we overcome this sense of the prison of society regularly. Those with criminal careers or intents do so with aplomb, though they fall into their own set of habits regarding their apparent lack of conscience for others, and sometimes stoic lack of concern for themselves. We may indeed feel as cousins of the criminal if we engage regularly in social sabotage. It has always been somewhat amusing to me that in psychological studies, the sociologist and the criminal show up next to each other on various personality scales. Even so, it is clear that:

> Authority is certainly not external compulsion, but rather that which has thoroughly permeated common customs, common practices, legislation, revolutions, and so forth and managed to resist the destructive force of criticism in such a way that it has ultimately been accepted by all the members of a society. (Gadamer 2004:85)

Here, "criticism" is used in the way we have been using the term "critique," as a reflective mode of being thoughtful about the world and oneself in it. The norms that go unquestioned in this way have always the potential to set themselves up as dogma, even nature, and cast their imposing edifices up on any human horizon. Usually in the form of institutions, these facades of meaningfulness can amplify any credo to the point of washing out thought itself.

George Orwell's now almost proverbial allegory *1984* speaks to this danger, a danger which, I believe, most of us are well aware. The theme of resistance, and even revolution itself in the face of dogma or fascism, is a popular entertainment commodity, whether the autonomy that is necessary for freedom be enlisted in the fight against alien invasion and domination, mental illness, peer pressure, institutional or governmental dictatorship, or even domestic abuse and tyranny. "Human freedom," however we may care to define it, is by its very invocation a phrase that connotes a "brand" of life to be consumed as well as an ideal to be defended. Gadamer further reminds us that "Anyone who is tempted to play on the institutional force of their authority rather than on genuine argument is always in danger of speaking in an authoritarian as opposed to an authoritative manner." (Gadamer 1996:124) This clears the space for a further distinction to be made between critique and criticism. The former always is ensconced within the dialogue and dialectic of argument, which may be questioned and discussed in reference to not only history in general but that of critique in particular, as well as with reference to one's own position in history. The latter often gives into the temptation of backing itself up with only the rule of what is encoded in law or even the quasi-legal apparatus all rationalized organizations — governments, corporations, educational systems, and so on — supply themselves with.

These home-grown versions of state constitutions and legal codes are enshrined in policy. To find one "going against policy" is to place oneself at risk. The whistleblower is only the most extreme case of resistance and critique in this area of life. It is notorious that however much the wider society or the public interest is served by such a person, their heroic defense of human freedom and justice is very much unappreciated by many more institutions than the one exposed. This is evidenced by the sudden lack of job opportunities such a person encounters after the moment of justice, and its correspondingly ironic fame, is passed. The true face of any organization committed to the obverse singular idols of either profit or power is also exposed when whatever smaller injustice that originally motivated the heroic engagement of critique comes to the surface.

That we mostly do not take up the resistance of critique in these areas of life speaks not so much to our own fragile bravery but rather to the powerful forces that can be enlisted in defense of political, corporate, or bureaucratic interest. Aside from the fetish of efficiency, the bottom line, and social order, there is the further embankment of general societal distrust of the whistleblower in any walk of life. All of us have our shadowy secrets, most of them picayune, perhaps, but even so we would rather not have brought to light. They may be moments or actions from our past, committed when we were less mature, or they may be ongoing foibles or even flaws that we have learned to artfully cover up in the presumably more polite company of our peers. Whatever their source, we in our own lives have some of the trappings of institutional structure, though writ small. In this sense, we are wary of the person to whom "nothing is sacred," the rebel or social critic, for example, or for that matter, perhaps the social scientist. The normative code of our society is not merely convenient for "getting along with the others," but also provides a comforting hostel to which we can return after committing our own private misdemeanors:

> So the "code fetishism," or nomolatry, of modern liberal society is potentially very damaging. It tends to forget the background which makes sense of any code: the variety of goods which the rules and norms are meant to realize, and it tends to make us insensitive, even blind, to the vertical dimension. It also encourages a "one size fits all" approach: a rule is a rule. One might even say

that modern nomolatry dumbs us down, morally and spiritually. (Taylor 2007:707)

It should not come as a surprise that criticism is itself addicted to the adoration of a code. The rules of this code follow the fashion of what certain social locations imagine is a righteous calling to critique, but due to precisely the effort to adhere to both a code and to remain within the peer group such a movement contrives to create, critique is soon abandoned for something more shallow. However radical the origin of the movement, once it becomes defined as indeed a "group," it betrays its own margins in much the same way it had accused the wider society of forsaking our own. This is to say that criticism also enjoys a doctrine, whereas critique never lets itself be boosted up onto a new pedestal. Thus is the irony, often tragic, of all revolutions in recent history and perhaps farther back in time. If we think, with the usual hindsight of the years that followed them, of 1917, 1949, and 1979 we are struck by the similarities of the sudden liberation from tyranny and thence the rather prompt establishment of tyranny anew. Russia, China, and Iran have, after their respective revolutions, not exactly enjoyed the freedoms imagined, or perhaps disingenuously promised, by their radical latter day founders. At the same time, and if we turn our gaze a little farther afield on our historical horizons, 1688, 1776, and 1789 appear also as revolutionary benchmarks. Although more to our taste in liberal Western society, perhaps some of the promises of the English, American, and French experiments in radical social change have yet to be fulfilled, at least for some of our fellow citizens. Whether writ large or small, and whether the change is societal or personal, what begins as promising—and in all of these six famous cases, no doubt empirically and ethically correct—critique, can rapidly descend to the artifact of the new rulers conjuring and enforcing their rules with as little regard for true freedom as had those they deposed. Such is the essence of quasi-charismatic authority, one may imagine. As previously suggested, we must return to Weber's understanding of the "routinization" of charisma, whether it is of a movement or more importantly, its ideas, to afford an explanation of why there is so often this sudden regression to the very thing that was abhorred.

It may well be a version, or resonance, of this historical dynamic that plays itself out in the personal shift from the radical alertness that at first proposes critique, to the convenient institution of new rules to follow and also thus new groups of people to follow these rules. Consider a common example from our own day. The world's largest retailer, Wal-Mart, is often the focus of what appears to be just and trenchant critique concerning its labor practices both at the source and supply ends. We are supposed to be shocked at the fact that developing world wages and working conditions are so marginal to what we have come to expect in our own locales. We rightly condemn the exploitation of child labor and the poverty line wages and lengthy work day hours of the labor of adults.

These situations remind us (perhaps more than anything, given that most of us have not actually visited these sites of "third world" production) of our high school history classes that focused on the industrial revolution in Europe from the 1730s to the 1870s. Indeed, a version of this kind of development is recurring elsewhere around the globe at this moment, and it feels like an almost "natural" development, whose pains of birth give forth, eventually, and at least for some people, the same vision of the "good society" to which we are loyal, and about which we discussed in the opening of this book. Here, the origins of the sense of injustice are in part historical, and thus suffer from the weakness of any historical analogy. Also, we are in fact most often either willing or semiconscious participants in the oppression of those exploited, whether around the corner on the streets of our hometowns, or across the globe in some seemingly exotic quarter where we would never dream of visiting, let alone imagining that we, too, through the bare and radical happenstance of birth, could take the place of those who so menially serve us. Already then, we have a potent and uncomfortable mix of *ressentiment*—here, exposed through the sense that we would be better than we are regarding the ethics of our consumptive practices—a somewhat murky acknowledgment of recent history, a murkier awareness of other cultures and their current status, and, finally, the apparent inability to act according to our own ideals, perhaps because they conflict with some of our other ideals. That is, our ideals concerning human freedom are at odds, in this instance and many others, with our ideas of convenience, efficiency, and consumption. In other words, our ideal of the good society contrasts with our idea of the good life.

This is, in essence, why what once was nascent critique becomes mere criticism, sharing the fate of revolutions of consciousness that occur on a much wider scale. The criticism of Wal-Mart, to return to the paragon example of this process in this setting, while correct insofar as all large corporations use the global labor market in as lucrative a way as possible for their own ends *and* for ours, does not take into account that on the supply end Wal-Mart has improved working conditions for a significant percentage of those who work in the service sector—students, working poor, retirees who are either bored or who themselves are impoverished, and some career management—and done so in stark contrast with other major minions of that consumer sector. Working conditions, wages, breaks, time off as paid vacation, other benefits, and even policy of the retail giant bear little resemblance to what passes for these items in other venues in the same sector. Every student that I have ever spoken with on this subject confirms that when compared to all other possibilities in working life in its incipience, Wal-

Mart by far outshines its competition. This is not say that these people wish to make a vocation of such a job, but it is a distinct amelioration of what is for now a necessity of life and work, and for some, a not very temporary one at that.

The source of the criticism of Wal-Mart is not merely only partially competent, it is disingenuous, because by far the majority of the members of its cadre hail from social locations that not only do not need to work there but can purchase their everyday items from much higher end retailers. On top of this, there is something else that the critics of Wal-Mart overlook, having most often never been in the position where they need to avail themselves of its presence. We often hear that the coming of Wal-Mart strikes a death knell for small town-businesses of many sorts. Yet we seldom hear of how small-town commerce functions to exclude the most vulnerable of its local populations from the ability to even purchase the necessities of life, or makes it much more difficult to do so, because of local practices of "fair competition." As far back as the mid-1950s, well before the advent of the superstores and fast food, Mills sardonically comments on the ideas of "fairness" that animates local business elites. The occluded facts surrounding the liberating quality of being able to find and possess, often for the first time, the goods that allow basic functioning to occur in the home and at work, need to be rendered in a brighter light. This new situation, where the margins of our society can now attain a certain and common dignity of quality of life is no small social achievement, even though we must admit that such is attained perhaps at the expense of yet others. That the middle classes and the professional intellectual elites, from whence the criticism of Wal-Mart inevitably flows, should be in sum saying to the less fortunate members of their society, *no, you should be ashamed for shopping there*, is to also say *you do not deserve what we, [through other processes of capital which are just as dubious or more so than Wal-Mart employs], can have.* Who should be ashamed here?

It should be clear that the essence of criticism is in the preservation of privilege, whether of material relations of your position, or of your ideas, or of your social status, and so forth. Critique, by contrast, objectively questions all positions and creates a standpoint that is in fact quite new to any of them, including the space where the critique begins. Critique employs both dialogue—in its ability to learn from other positions—and dialectic, in its ability to engage each of these in a focused and critical manner. Criticism can accomplish neither, due to its unreflective loyalty to its own position. When this is coupled by the often mixed competencies of its arguments, and the conflicting ideals of its ethics, the result is merely another interested but hypocritical voice in the chorus of unthought that dominates our current public debates.

This discussion, though apparently public, does not really speak for society as a whole. The shoppers and workers at Wal-Mart are not represented by those who are critical of them, for example. As Gadamer says,

> ... one must do more than advance the public discussion. One must also do something oneself; and indeed one is already doing something [right or wrong]. Praxis, however, means to act, and that starts with an alert consciousness. Conscious action is more than just something. A human being is one who controls himself or herself. This involves, self-control, self-testing, and setting an example. (Gadamer 2001:82)

Evaluating oneself in a critical manner, without unnecessary derogation, and without the trappings of a shallow criticism borrowed from the fashion or media standards of the day—*How do I look? Am I too fat?* and so on— need not be Augustinian in its scope and perhaps neurosis to be effective. Such an effect auto-critique has is the realization of character. This is not the kind of character we are supposed to admire in novels concerning morality, but the awareness that our character is both human and must become humane. We set examples with everything we do, especially if we are in charge of children. So doing and being are here set up in contraposition. The "mode of being neighborly," for instance, is a manner of living that is not mere lifestyle, and yet is not entirely conscious of itself in that its apparently most gracious acts are spontaneous and uncalculated, like the immediate response of the "good Samaritan." Merely "doing something," as in the above quote, is what we do most of the time—rendering spontaneous aid in a sudden crisis may mark the heroic character in our humanity with some definition, but it is a rare event when compared with all of the action we must take in life that requires us to be alert and engage in self-critique. Thinking before doing, or as part of our doing, is part of the ongoing process of all forms of critique. The casual idiom "look before you leap" expresses part of this situation. Yet, critique also must not carry itself into the abstract at the expense of its reference, the world as it is, lest it become beholden to desire and uncritical wish-fulfillment. Speaking of Lessing to this regard, Arendt tell us that,

> His attitude toward the world was neither positive nor negative, but radically critical and, in respect to the public realm of his time, completely revolutionary. But it was also an attitude that remained indebted to the world, never left the solid ground of the world, and never went to the extreme of sentimental utopianism. (Arendt 1968:5)

Critique abandons its service to the wider community and humankind as a whole when it finds itself enthralled to either personal or even local feelings of want or desire. One must rather be vigilant to at once not remake the self in the

Criticism and Critique

service of what we may think others wish of us, nor through our criticism push others to be as we wish.

At its source, the demand for critique emanates from ethics. In the same way, the source of the demand for silence is most often found where critique would expose injustice and inhumanity. Such a relationship is, however, often masked by utility, and even perhaps surprisingly, other human feelings that we generally associate with awe, wonder, curiosity, and even bravery. The use value of modern knowledge often insulates it against critique. Yet, at the same time, the wonders revealed by the combination of scientific acumen and technological prosthesis leave us in silent awe. This feeling is necessary for mortal beings who confront a seemingly infinite universe, and reminds us of our humanity in a way few other situations can match. Yet, such wonder can be addicting. We may attempt to place ourselves in such a situation again and again, without regard to other human costs, or the always questionable distribution of resources in modern global capital:

> In truth, modern science represents an impressive embodiment of critical freedom that is to be marvelled at. But we should also be aware of the human demand that is placed on all those who personally participate in this authority: the demand for self-discipline and self-criticism, and this is an ethical demand. (Gadamer 1996:122)

Knowledge is always, from the beginning, human knowledge of ourselves within the cosmos. We cannot pretend that here is something called "knowledge for its own sake," although my own vocation ironically attempts to purvey this idea of knowing to students and others, in order to allay the anxiety surrounding their quest for a habitable place in the job market and a tolerable life in the market society. Rather, knowledge is always "knowledge for something." This is reflected in some of our oldest mythic narratives that speak of the birth of human knowledge. In Genesis, of course, we are told that the enlightenment regarding the human condition—the beginning of the truly human endeavor of cultural adaptation, survival, and gradual and halting growth in both our knowledge and our character—has everything to do with not a "tree of knowledge," but a the "tree of knowledge of good and evil." Right from the earliest accounts we have the sense that to know something as humans is to also participate in the value of its knowledge. Knowing, for us, means also valuing. Knowledge itself has a value of some kind, and can immediately be used to act in the world. Given this, it very much matters just what kind of "something" knowledge is to be used for, and perhaps more importantly, it also matters very much the source of its valuation. Although the modern mind may scoff at the mythic proportions of the narratives of human cosmogony, it in fact is clear that all possibility of authentic critique stems from the valuation of knowledge.

That original critique, embodied in the Jewish narrative amongst many others, is merely an archetypical allegory for what we humans must engage in. Yahweh casts the first humans out because he is critical of their decision—not to know something in general, but the use to which such knowledge is immediately put and thus the corresponding lack of perspective it momentarily generates. Such a decision on the part of Yahweh communicates in the most effective manner the need, in all human situations, of taking into account the whole—or at least as much of the whole that mortal beings can at any one time in their history grasp; hence again the need for the other to self—rather than merely dwelling on what is convenient. Being sent out into the world, aside from being a larger-than-life allegory of the parent demanding that the child make his or her own way in the world—still a rite of passage in our society some thousands of years later—is the most obvious way to enlighten human beings about their true condition. We do not live in a paradise where all is immediately present for us. We must think ourselves through sometimes the most petty of situations, as well as ponder and puzzle our way around those more profound. We do this within the knowledge of the immanence of death in life, and we live so only in so far as we are ignorant of the exact timing of that mortality, rehearsing at various levels the final curtain call through the diverse farewells of social life. The unadulterated joy in the garden, akin to the non-responsibility of childhood, suddenly and radically gives way to the heavy obligation of the world as it is, adulthood instead of childhood, human union instead of divine communion, and work or die rather than a leisured immortality. Nietzsche comments on this transition in his epigram "you who have said yes to one joy, do you not know that you have thus said yes to all sorrows as well?"

Of course, we need not pine the loss of the mythic garden if we indeed had a long enough and blissful enough childhood there. True, many, perhaps most, children in all cultures do not find their tenure in paradise all that it should have been, and we spend much energy trying to make up for this loss later in life. Many of us find, to our chagrin or worse, that what is missed as a child cannot be had as an adult, whether it be the time needed to be without obligations of any serious kind, or the open heart necessary for various forms of intimacy both erotic and filial. Being evicted from paradise is a profound moment in the history of all human beings, and we are tempted to say that the later this inevitability occurs, the better. Some few of us—wealthy elites whose abilities rest on their fellow humans in a peculiarly onerous manner—attempt to postpone receipt of their eviction notice until the day that other notice of eviction in human life appears. This attempt artificially makes what are really two phases of human mortality and its evolution into one thing. Whereas we are aware of the growth—personal, scientific, ethical, and spiritual—needed to become fully human and thence to become humane, in collapsing living and dying as one thing annuls the necessary tension involved in having to *learn something* and *value something* in the time allotted. The awareness of one's own finitude, of which Gadamer makes a primary characteristic of human maturity, gives the principle for the value of living on in general, as well as the ability to understand the value of human knowledge in whatever particular incidence it may arise and be used. Feigning ignorance of this fundamental bond, perhaps pretending that it itself is only a form of bondage, is to ignore uncritically the human condition not only as it is, but is to imagine that one is aloof to "all of the sorrow" and indeed, much of the joy as well, that animates what it means to be human in the world. Those who participate in this materially elite theater of living also help to condemn the weakest of humanity to the material margins.

Yet it is not only scientific and historical knowledge and its evaluation and use that are to be critiqued. The rather different species of knowledge that comes from faith is also not to be held apart from its place in the human condition, and not to be valued uncritically or to become the home of mere criticism of others: "None of us stands at the point of view of the universal. Our attachment to our own faith cannot come from a universal survey of all others from which we conclude that this is the right one. It can only come from our sense of its inner spiritual power, chastened by the challenge which we will have had to meet from other faiths." (Taylor 2007:680) And not only is this kind of knowledge given perspective on itself from other forms of knowledge that may have the same aspirations and modes of valuation in them, but also that of rational and scientific knowing, ethical experience through living, and the power of aesthetic experience which all come into play. Indeed, all of us must become as lay philosophers, for it is that kind of universal perspective that emanates from life itself that is ultimately both at stake and necessary in understanding such a stake. As Grondin iterates, ". . . the question of philosophy, how is truth possible, can be raised with regard to all possible truths, but philosophy must ask in the same breath how these various truths relate to each other. Thus its activity is necessarily *systematic*." (Grondin 2003:65; italics in the original)

The various modes of knowing the human condition then are in the service of the same kind of truth, the truth about being human. This is not an ultimate truth, and neither is it objective. But at the same time it is not pure subjectivity. Human truths are constructed through socialization and the maintenance of social reality, change over time in all of their venues, and thus can be changed at any particular time and place. Even so, they are massively real to us, and the knowledge that the human situation can be changed radically and suddenly does not necessarily detract from their power. Yet it is only when we give into their reality as indeed ultimate that we lose sight of their true character. Human truths are profound precisely because they are mutable and subject to critique. It is an impressive feat that our species has been able to accomplish what we have, and what we are, with no access to the objective truth of things. Such a vision cannot exist for finite beings, whether or not it exists in a separate ontological status somewhere in the wider cosmos, with a God perhaps, or with a more evolved form of life in general. That we can know the cosmos in a relatively ordered manner and explore our "nature" within it remains the most important feature of our existence. To lose this ability by either engaging in mere criticism or by excerpting ourselves from the confrontation with tradition—

knowledge and truth as it has been known to us both as persons and as the diversity of cultures within a species—is to effectively lose our humanity. That it is understandable how we might be tempted to turn away from such a task, given what is produced by such critique and confrontation, is also part of the self-understanding of the human project. The awe and wonder we feel within our knowledge of the cosmos, and which sometimes can distract us from the task of both critique and justice, is paired with a concern and even an anxiousness with regard to the fragile nature of human knowledge and being:

> The anthropological basis of anxiety testifies to a specifically human characteristic, that is, that a person has a distance from their own self. Heidegger saw in this the inauthenticity of an existence permanently absorbed in life, and contrasted it with an authentic existence which is prepared to face anxiety. But this inauthenticity also belongs to human nature. (Gadamer 1996:157)

Criticism is part of the turning inward of living. We see in others what we disdain in ourselves, or versions thereof, and the ease by which this ability to cast aspersion on the other comes to us gives us the feeling that we are ourselves at ease, that we can be at home in the world even though that world is the object of our disdain. One becomes "absorbed" right at this point. The attention we project on the other and the attempt we make to make that person into a kind of denied self, a surrogate for our lack of self-reflection, and an expectation that even after the withering storm of insult, that this other can still serve us in our lack of self-understanding, is certainly both arrogant and uncritical. But further to this, such an engagement of criticism allays the anxiety that must accompany all true risking of what we are. To know an other as a truly different human being, rather than a guise of ourselves or some other more material servant, is to consistently and constantly risk the self. Naturally, this produces an anxiety that cannot be tempered with the knowledge that we can always return to what we had left. Indeed, this feeling of leaving home is part of the anxiety of understanding the other. We know, in the authentic encounter with existence within the human community, that when we do return to ourselves, that which was the being we knew is no more. We have been changed by the encounter with the other—they too have changed in some way but we may not necessarily be aware of the precise implications of this for the other—and thus our return is never prodigal. We do not "come back" in any regular sense of that phrase. Rather, and perhaps this is the most pressing characteristic of this kind of anxiety, what we encounter in our changed self is yet another otherness. This time, however, we must call this otherness our own and inhabit it; there is nowhere else to go, after all.

So it is understandable, given the radicality of not merely the other to self as it stands, but the strangeness of "returning" to a place where in fact one has not yet ever been until that moment that we shy away from really placing ourselves in the hands of otherness. Better, we feel, to walk through life not getting too close to people or too reflective about ideas, or without engaging in too much critique concerning ourselves or our society. We would rather wish and yet be careful what we wish for. We do not want to "get it" in the sense that we must confront the anxiety that surely is also our own by our very nature as finite beings in an apparently infinite universe. Yet in spite of both these trepidations—their inauthenticity, as Gadamer suggested, is also very much a part of us and thus cannot itself be disdained in any petty way—and as well in spite of overcoming them, there is a part of us that can become resilient and open to otherness both within and without ourselves. What we can call humaneness is the result of the dialogue with the other to self, and the dialectic of risk and return that characterizes all authentic encounters in these spheres. Our ancestors knew its import, and

> By that they meant something which was the very height of humanness because it was valid without being objective. It is precisely what Kant and Jaspers mean by *Humanitat*, the valid personality which, once acquired, never leaves a man, even though all other gifts of body and mind may succumb to the destructiveness of time. *Humanitas* is never acquired in solitude and never by giving one's work to the public. It can be achieved only by one who has thrown his life and his person into the "venture into the public realm"—in the course of which he risks revealing something which is not "subjective" and which for that very reason he can neither recognize nor control. [This] becomes a gift to mankind. (Arendt 1968:73–74)

A full humanity, with its ethical aspect humaneness, is possible if we give ourselves without reserve to that space where the distinction between our private understanding of the world we have created for ourselves and the world as it is, populated by radical alters to self and to the private, mingles and becomes indistinct. It is only through the journey with the other that we come home to what we are now. What we have been is transformed by what the other may be. This is yet another reason why critique is practiced in the full presence of risk, as it calls into question our very existence. Only through doing so is it able to be radical in its questioning of the world, for we are indeed part of that very world that is to be questioned in this manner. Human beings cannot exempt themselves from living in the world. All criticism can do is to objectify the world of negative desire while at the same time suppressing the self's true relationship with the world as it is. We disdain the other because they do not measure up to some desired image of the self, and we do so specifically in order to exempt the self from reflective query. Objectification—the treating of the other as if he or she were only a thing or a projection of an aspect of what is thing-like in ourselves—allows us to object to the idea that the other is in fact another human being.

We can also object to the knowledge that in order to get on with life, we often have to change ourselves. The world does not wait for us. The world will move on without us if we remain unchanged by its wonder and its mystery. Criticism can delay what is inevitable for all thinking beings, and sometimes it can provide an addiction within which one can hide from the world. Ultimately, however, mere criticism has no power over the other. The other is not changed by our negative desires and must in turn be forced to object to them. We in turn are stagnated by such a practice, as the objection of the other comes back to us with the message that the other resists our very attempts at objectification—and thus the vicious circle continues. This false dialectic takes place between persons as it occurs between cultures or nations. The end result of long-term criticism without reflection is often the sense that we must kill the other to have our desire come true in the world, thereby depriving ourselves, the others, and the world of a full humanity.

Critique, rather, avoids all of these problems by including within its orbit the self that is to be changed. Dialogue opens up the spirit of reflective risk with the trust that the other will be ready to embark on the life-changing course of encounter with another and the confrontation with tradition. Dialectic results from the sheer otherness that is presented to both parties by one another's presence in the world. Finally, the new knowledge of what all this means to both of us becomes itself an object for further exploration and reflection: "For the world is not humane just because it is made by human beings, and it does not become humane just because the human voice sounds in it, but only when it has become the object of discourse." (ibid:24)

This discourse is the embodiment of the dual character of critique. Dialogue and dialectic are necessary partners. It is also the reflection of the dual direction of critique. Both *self* and *other* are to be questioned by history and the world, what human knowledge has been and what it is today, and both at the same time question each other and themselves. The fact that we cannot control or predict the outcomes of these examinations is part of the risk. This may be disconcerting and enervating but it remains a necessity. We have already seen that criticism attempts to control the other by forcing him to conform to our ideals or desires in the world. It also controls the self by forcing it to remain static in the face of a diverse and changing world. Yet its most important facade lies in its ability to pretend that we know the outcomes of our engagement with the other and with the world, that we can predict with utter facility and facileness what will occur when we pass our judgments. Knowledge cannot be had from such a mockery of the human condition. Information, yes, perhaps, but knowledge, let alone wisdom, requires that we put at risk what we think we know. That alone puts criticism out of court, because it is all about conserving ourselves against all forms of risk and otherness. It is precisely because we do not and cannot know the results of interaction with the world in the ongoing lives of human beings that we are to gain knowledge. This is the "reward," if you will, for the risk of losing what has passed for prior knowledge:

> We are in fact all thinking, and feeling out of backgrounds and frameworks which we do not fully understand. To ascribe total personal responsibility to us for these is to want to leap out of the human condition. At the same time, no background leaves us utterly without room for movement and change. The realities of human life are messier than is dreamed of either by dogmatic rationalists, or in the Manichean rigidities of embattled orthodoxy. (Taylor 2007:387)

No doubt we are all, sometime or often, scared of change in general, let alone changes with intimately personal implications. The most radical changes in human life call forth the most stress and danger from within us. It is no surprise to recall that the most stressful situations, where people report the most anxiety and where they retreat most fully from the course of life and the movement of the world, are when we lose a loved one, especially a partner or spouse, and then, secondly, when we lose the means of subsistence, our jobs or vocations. This makes complete sense to us because we realize that in both of these losses the bonds to the two most important aspects of human life are fundamentally broken. In the one we lose community, and in the second we lose physicality. The former gives us our human spirit, while the latter provides the healthy space where such a spirit may reside and grow. To place these at sudden risk through critique is not to extinguish them but rather to help them both in that very and necessary growth. Critique is not abandonment but it's very opposite. We appropriately must wince at forms of life that make real the immanence of death. Yet critique represents such an immanence metaphorically—we do know that we are about to lose something of ourselves, but we are ready to do so. We are never truly ready to lose community and to lose our means of subsistence and health. Yet even here, most people bounce back from such losses in a way that is uniquely human and perhaps shows us at our most courageous and noble. In the face of sudden death and loss, human life goes on, and the knowledge of this keeps us going. We also, in the midst of realizing changes and new knowledge, are apprised of the ongoing fact that the world, so imposing and forceful and apparently larger than life, is indeed amenable to positive change and to questioning. The world is our world after all, even if it be not entirely our own.

Pessimism and Skepticism

IT IS easy to get down about the world. It often seems that the most realistic view of the human condition is a negative one. There is the present: All we have to do is think about conflict, poverty, fanaticism, environmental degradation, nuclear weapons proliferation, political corruption, crime, and economic depressions and recessions and we feel badly. There is the past: warfare, political competition and empires of colonialism, genocide and world war, slavery and pillory—and we wince at the thought of human history. There is the structural: social injustice and inequality, gender and power inequities, racial and ethnic inequalities, declining standards of health and health care, *ressentiment* and religious intolerances, even hatreds—and we close our eyes in disbelief. And there is the personal: mental illness, jealousy, misdirected anger, unethical desires, unconcernful action in the day to day, and domestic abuse and other abuses—and we begin to lose hope. All of these things, and all of the levels of consciousness that hail from, are very real, we say, and thus is it not most realistic to in fact be pessimistic about both the human present and perhaps even more so, our collective future?

There is no getting around the fact that a realistic accounting of the human condition as it stands, and as it has perhaps stood for about ten thousand years or so, would have to take into account all these factors and many more to be truthful about its subject matter. Like unbridled optimism, however, a solely pessimistic interpretation of who we are and what we have done — to the earth and to each other — cannot ever be entirely realistic, as its primary sense leaves out, by definition, its alter, the positive. It is also a fact, for example, that most human action and even most of the ideas we dream up have both good and bad effects, positive and negative outcomes, very often simultaneously. There are few instances of transparent evil in the world without resistance to evil. There are few moments of immediate and whole-souled good in the world, without someone peddling an ulterior motive under the guise of the good.

It is said that a clear conscious makes for the softest pillow. I am writing this at four in the morning — does this mean that my personal history or my personal present weighs heavily upon me? Could it be that I am escaping some other task that ethically demands my attention? Or might I just be excited about my work, thrilled to once again approach a new text, a new chapter, and feel that I have something or other to say with it? Perhaps I do not wish to disturb my wife, whom I have left in bed, with my nocturnal musings? Perhaps I have other more, indeed, even ethically more, things to accomplish during the daylight hours of the morrow? It is likely that much of our day-to-day lives are filled with events and actions, even intents and thoughts that bear equally the possibility of bright or shadowy import, and very likely the possibility of both. Human life is nothing if not ambiguous in its ethical demonstration, and over the long-term, even within the course of a human lifespan, it does not bear the wholly pessimistic or optimistic interpretation.

It is fair to judge the optimist as often naive about the ways of the world. The Dutch, the inventors of capitalism, used to practice a small rite of passage for their children. They needed a way to decide whether or not their children knew enough of the world to let them roam in it unsupervised. They offered a small child either an apple or a penny. If the child took the apple he or she stayed in the house, but if they took the penny, they were free to leave and walk the streets of the town, for they knew what the world was about. Not an unrealistic test, we might argue, though it might also sound a little simplistic to us today, who are in somewhat different circumstances than the seventeenth century Dutch. Perhaps it might even sound a little cynical. However the case may be, it is clear that every parent must make a similar kind of decision, and the variables that come into play are highly influenced by our prevailing view of the "ways of the world." Giving over the education of our children to institutions sometimes only heightens the anxiety. The tension between imagining that children need to be sheltered from the horrors of human life and the awareness that as children grow, their very growth depends on knowing as intimately as possible all of the corners of the human condition, no matter how shady, promotes ambiguity indeed in not merely our decision-making concerning children's autonomy but our feelings about their place in the future of this world. Perhaps some of us have given up, either saying "let the schools or society take are of it," "everything will work itself out naturally in due course," or even "just get them an Internet connection and let them loose." Yet we are aware that even in this day of alternative family structure and massive media and fashion saturation, children are still "our own" in a unique way. Perhaps more so now than at any other time in human history, our children "belong" to us as individuals, and not to community of any kind, for better or worse. We tend to be shy of letting them belong to anything larger for a certain period of their youth, lest our influence be muted and forgotten. The emotions of loss, mourning, even resentment, and perhaps yet even sexual jealousy when they move away, find partners or get married, ascend to career heights we ourselves never dreamed of, lose "their" religion, or change their politics are a negative testament to the enduring bonds that make the filial relation so powerful. Our pride and our concern for them as they accomplish their goals of struggle to overcome their deficits is the positive testament to the same thing. Our sorrow at their losses, our mourning if they are killed in war or in crime or even by the happenstance of health, speaks profoundly of an enduring human bond that most societies consider to be sacred. Yet, in spite of all of this interest and the reality that it seeks to promote, we are made painfully aware that the situations the world presents to our children are often beyond our control, sometimes apparently beyond our comprehension, as social and technological change leaves us behind in the worlds we have taken for granted.

The ever-present temptation in our modern society is to seek expert advice when our own has run dry. After all, we reason, our children have been in the hands of experts since the beginning. From birth in medical facilities to schools of various kinds and levels, perhaps to colleges or professional apprenticeships, the passing on of expertise is a dynamic that most of us today have been born into. If we encounter problems later on it not only seems to make sense to call in an expert but, more than this, it has long since become a habit, even a structural circumstance. Yet we are somehow aware that reliance on experts in the wider sense of the social fabric and community to which we belong or at least adhere means giving up something. For whatever advice or technique we gain, we do so at the cost of our own reflective practice and our own sense of what we can ourselves accomplish in the world. This tension is often imposed upon us, and not merely because there are far too many circles of life about which we know nothing. It is simply more convenient, given our own responsibilities, to give over the power of reflective practice, or *praxis*, to another who supposedly is more skilled than us at that very practice. Max Weber argued strenuously against doing so. There is some irony here, perhaps, given that he is arguably the greatest expert on society that has ever lived, warning us incessantly not to rely on the experts for any question that really matters. Weber was loyal to a philosophical tradition that saw reason at the very heart of human consciousness, and thus also to the idea that every human being could only become fully human through its active exercise. In the following interview, we see that Gadamer shares this profound notion of who and what we are:

Dutt: Of course one does not find in your thought the pessimism that predominates in the late texts of Adorno and Horkheimer. The gesture of your texts is different from this. You are more confident.

Gadamer: Yes, I am very skeptical of every kind of pessimism. I find in all pessimism a certain lack of sincerity.

Dutt: Why?

Gadamer: Because no one can live without hope.

Dutt: But express hope, of course, does not mean that you join the chorus of philosophers of cheer.

Gadamer: Most certainly not! Naturally one cannot keep quiet about the negative.

Dutt: You have warned very strongly against the undermining of reason in society through the false ideals held by a society full of experts and functionaries.

Gadamer: Oh, yes, here lies a danger which we really have to keep continually in mind, and which we must energetically work against! Of course, in the highly technologized industrialized society in which we live the expert is a phenomenon that we would certainly not wish away. Experts have become indispensable in the most varied realms, in order

> to assure the requisite management and control of complex theoretical and technical processes. But it is an error to think that "the experts"—the business and economic experts, the environmental experts, or the military experts—can take away from us our praxis in society and relieve us from decisions on matters we all have to deal with as political citizens working with each other, matters that we all have to face and deal with. (Gadamer 2001:83)

If we do give over our obligations and our rights to an elite few who then make decisions on behalf of all of us, we give over our power as human beings to shape our lives and the history into which we have been born. Yet even this, as negative as it sounds, is in fact too optimistic. Elite groups of decision-makers, experts or not, do *not* in fact tend to make decisions on others' behalf but only on behalf of either themselves, if they are at the centers of power, or on behalf of those powerful interests that have paid them to decide on *their* behalf. So there is a double jeopardy here: On the one hand we give up power in good faith, which in terms of a society of experts is still an error and makes our humanity less than it could be, and on the other hand, we have given up our power to those who wield it unscrupulously with no regard to ourselves. Perhaps the second follows from the first. In any case, we are aware, even in our personal and perhaps private lives, that when one human being surrenders to another some part of their life, the potential for abuse of the newfound power by another human being undergoes sudden magnification. Given that we are all controlled by quite dense and hardly impartial structures and institutions during our primary socialization, it is germane to think that we will be tempted by opportunities later in life to control others. Some of us our bred for such control, as it is well known in the sociology of education that children of elites are taught in a very different manner than are the children of workers. These latter are taught to conform and obey, to "follow orders" — the men and women of the SS and Gestapo, for example, were culled from these social classes — while the former are taught to think problems through, to question authority in order to remake it, and to practice the performance of issuing authorities of all kinds. Pessimism and perhaps fatalism are the results of an authoritarian pedagogy that simply demands obedience, while skepticism is the first order of the day for a questioning pedagogy. The fact that this elite way of learning often turns those to whom obedience is demanded to cynicism ought to give us pause, and is a clue to the potential corruption of power that has made Acton's remark about it one of the most famous in history.

Given that there are few elites, by definition, and there are masses of the rest of us, the import of Weber's (and Gadamer's) warnings become all the more clear. If we are taught only unquestioning obedience we have no imagination for skeptical inquiry. If we are taught to perform and maintain power, then that set of goals becomes an absolute value, and such questioning that does occur is harnessed to instrumental purposes. Open questions that leave the spaces of social life vulnerable to further questions are not permitted in either the elite or the mass ways of learning. True skepticism is inconvenient for both, because it inevitably exposes oppression for the masses and manipulation for the elites. More than this, skepticism in day-to-day life is lost to the idea that thinking actually involves criticism (in the above sense) and emotion, pessimism (or optimism), belief and desire. Here is another "dialogue" from Sagan's final book:

> I'm frequently asked, "Do you believe there's extraterrestrial intelligence?" I give the standard arguments—there are a lot of places out there, the

molecules for life are everywhere, I use the word *billions*, and so on. Then I say it would be astonishing to me if there weren't extraterrestrial intelligence, but of course there is yet no compelling evidence for it.

Often, I'm asked next, "What do you really think?"

I say, "I just told you what I really think."

"Yes, but what's your gut feeling?"

But I try not to think with my gut. If I'm serious about understanding the world, thinking with anything besides my brain, as tempting as that might be, is likely to get me into trouble. Really, it's okay to reserve judgement until the evidence is in. (Sagan 1996:180; italics in the original)

What is called thinking by purported institutional sources thereof is something of which we can remain highly skeptical. Are there not ulterior motives at stake when we demand of only our institutions to instruct us in the arts of thought? There are many other sources to help us in this human vision quest: the history of discourse, lived experience, the experiences of others who are perhaps older and more experienced than ourselves, and observation of the world as it is. Yet we are also aware, due precisely to the society of expertise that we have set up along with our modern mode of production and its attendant rationalized processes that accessing the means to begin to discover all of these extra-institutional sources of thought lie ironically in the institutions themselves. Doctorates in sociology, philosophy, or astronomy are not handed out in the streets, as it were. So how do we maintain something that we have never been exposed to? Our good faith can be muted when we commit our children to educational bureaucracies only to find out that the true intent of those who inhabit them is to reproduce themselves, and, as often as not, this never involves serious critique or skeptical inquiries of any kind.

Teachers of all types and levels in fact often use individualistic narrative to make their claims and underscore their points because they know this is popular with students and children. Each year in my introductory sociology class I know ahead of time that I will receive at least a few unhappy rebuttals to the claims of social science that rest on the biographical experience of the student. It is tempting to destroy such claims outright, but this is both unethical and pedagogically ineffective. Nevertheless, one errs from time to time and my favorite moment of temptation simply occurred when I mentioned that the total divorce rate for those married before the age of twenty-five was 85 percent (as it was for a time in North America), that is to say, if one married young you had an only 15 percent chance of staying together for the duration. One young female student objected strenuously, saying that her parents were high school sweethearts who had married at eighteen, and were still together at fifty or so. *Congratulate them*, I sardonically replied, *they are part of the 15 percent*. As petty as my reply was, it does serve to exemplify the ability we humans have to take our own experience and project it, uncritically, into the world. The world as it is, however, is not beholden to most persons' desires, and is only yet partially enthralled to the desires of the powerful. But human thinking is not at its best when it accedes to the desires of any of us, rich or poor, as it ultimately breeds an inability to think with appropriate candor and skepticism at all. Popular culture knowledge of UFOs and the like are a famous current example of this problem:

> No anecdotal claim—no matter how sincere, no mater how deeply felt, no matter how exemplary the lives of the attesting citizens—carries much weight on so important a question. As in the older UFO cases, anecdotal accounts are subject to irreducible error. This is not a personal criticism of those who say they've been

abducted or of those who interrogate them. It is not tantamount to contempt for purported witnesses. It is not—or should not be—arrogant dismissal of sincere and affecting testimony. It is merely a reluctant response to human fallibility. (Sagan 1996:180–81)

Where there are powerful structural forces at work in our lives—the influence of media and the suspicion of large organizations such as corporations and governments, for example—we are that much more likely to attend to our anxieties and aspirations regarding what appears as either threatening or redeeming. The phenomenon of UFO religions attests to both our longing for some kind of egress from not only our worldly existential state but from the state of a world so often disappointing or even horrifying, as well as our fears about some source of these tribulations being not even human. The impoverishment we feel ourselves to be in when facing such problems is, I think, the most likely source of our interest in them. That these kinds of problems and our emotional reactions to them are ancient and have long motivated religious beliefs of all kind is also well known. Though religion is often used as a rationalization, a complex excuse, for taking action based on other motives not at all religious let alone ethical may also be part of what is at stake when we trade skepticism for pessimism:

> In the early 1960s, I argued that UFO stories were crafted chiefly to satisfy religious longings. At a time when science has complicated uncritical adherence to the old-time religions, an alternate is proffered to the God hypothesis. Dressed in scientific jargon, their immense powers "explained" by superficially scientific terminology, the gods and demons of old come down from heaven to haunt us, to offer prophetic visions, and to tantalize us with visions of a more hopeful future; a space-age mystery religion aborning. (ibid:130)

We are very much aware that, as Gadamer suggested above, we are more often sentenced to accept our situations than to have direct and utter control over them. We are socialized into this ability to accept these contexts as children, no matter what culture we hail from. Coercion is the hallmark of all childhoods, perhaps even more than is non-responsibility. We learn to coerce ourselves "voluntarily" to perform the roles and scripts of a large sociality. We can withhold our cooperation, of course, but there are often consequences, sometimes serious ones. We are always present to the temptation of imagining that we have no actual choices and that we must do what the larger community, or even bureaucracy, expects of us. This is never truly the case, as the American sociologist and religious scholar Peter Berger poignantly reminded us in the above, citing Sartre's famous definition of "bad faith." Once again, to be in bad faith has nothing to do with a heretical moral belief but rather consists of pretending that one has no choice but do take this or that action when in fact the constraints acting against the feeling of free will and the choices that must emanate from it are simple limitations of the roles we happen to be playing at the time. If I follow the rules of the social role of both professor and husband, certain eventualities will never occur. In this case, I agree with those rules and think that they circumscribe ethical action and proscribe that unethical. But I might not always agree with the rules of certain roles—the idea that the "good citizen" does not question the nation state's authority, for example—and hence I must not pretend that I, in wishing to break the rules, cannot do so because of some existential imperative. Sartre famously argues that "bad faith" helps us to avoid the "agony of choice" and that we are "condemned" by our very nature to freedom (cf. especially chapter six of Berger 1963). The idea that we play our social roles consciously and reflectively, and critique them and be critiqued by their history and the social contexts of their enactment, is in fact to be skeptical of both their force and their moral suasion. To allow them to control us as if we were not ultimately free—even though we know there are sometimes daunting consequences for stepping outside our social roles—is to breed a kind of fatalism that has its escape in criticism and pessimism. The most challenging aspect of stepping out of role constraints is of course not so much that others will react but that we ourselves are forced to engage in ethics, rather than simply accept the dominant or fashionable morality of the time and place. To do so is to place oneself at risk, and to realize the true separation of most of the conceptual tandems discussed so far in this book. Pessimism sometimes seems so close to skepticism that it may be difficult to tell them apart, but examination of the evidence that our feelings then refract is a good start. More reflectively, we can be aware of the historical situation of humankind in general: "In particular, we can consider the skepticism of science woven into . . . hermeneutics, its emphasis on the negative character of all genuine experience, and also its theses concerning the eccentric quality of human subjectivity, which rather suffers its fate than controls it." (Grondin 2003:57)

One of the effects of thinking like this, rather than accepting without skepticism the fashionable accounts of human history and its recent trends to individuation, is that we are less able to be pessimistic about the outcomes of its trajectories, whether their horizon is near or far. Realism, the outcome of skeptical thought allied with simple observation and the taking into account the self-understanding that comes from lived experience, suggests that we in fact ought also to be impressed positively with our accomplishments, in spite of the knowledge of their darker sides. Not that we in the West should, as the Victorians apparently officially did until late in their era, be constantly patting ourselves on the back for actuating "eternal progress" and "manifest destiny." That kind of willing naivety, based on empire and racism amongst other things, is now at least—equally officially perhaps—seen as immoral and unjust, as well as being empirically incorrect, given the rise of Asian economic power. The idea that we have gradually whittled away at the previous mode of thinking and living to expose our true nature, rational, progressive, and tolerant, is, at best, another official story we tell ourselves to ostensibly give us the sense that we need not be so pessimistic about the human future. Taylor, for one, is very skeptical of this narrative, and the critique he brings to it is one of the major themes of his recent book. The idea that we can gain an egress from pessimism by rehabilitating the idea of progress from its demise in the First World War in fact hides a more important recognition:

> The subtraction story doesn't allow us to be as surprised as we ought to be at this achievement—or as admiring of it; because it is after all one of the great realizations in the history of human development, whatever our ultimate views about its cope and limitations.... It is an achievement, because getting to the point of where we can be inspired by an impartial view of things, or a sense of buried sympathy within, requires training, or inculcated insight, and frequently much work on ourselves. It is in this respect like being moved by other great moral sources in our tradition, be they the idea of the Good, or God's agape, or the Tao, or human-heartedness. These things are not just given to us by birth... Making the new sources available was thus a step in an unprecedented direction, something not to be dismissed lightly. (Taylor 2007:255)

It is not the very first time, of course, that we as humans have imagined our humanity in this particularly naked way, without gods or demons, without ultimate or singular purposes. Originally, we imagine that this was the way in which humanity began the slow evolution from proto-hominid primate beings to ourselves. The key shift is that with the advent of the social contract, this evolution became *cultural*. Humanity unhinged itself to a great extent from its own biological substrate. That we are finding out today more clearly where we stand as thinking social beings over against our own physical makeup is something necessary for the species' self-understanding to further itself. We are literally "under the gun" in this venture, as we are often too well aware, whether the barrel of that gun is simply ecological or whether it is thermonuclear is somehow secondary. But the fact that human beings came together in a unique way to survive in a dangerous and dominant nature has changed only in the sense that our own "nature" has added to the suite of risks associated with long-term survival. The pessimist would argue that this addition has made things worse for us and for the world, for whatever we do negatively also impacts the rest of life on earth in a negative manner, at least over the longer term. This position, however, sees only an aspect of the situation, one that perhaps is fraught with the most tension, but one that does not have a monopoly on either outcomes or processes. We may indeed be skeptical about our future, but that we can imagine a future is of utmost import, even, and perhaps especially, when we can imagine the apocalypse of total war or environmental breakdown. Skepticism only points out the likely realities of certain processes and suggests probabilities for their outcomes; it is not certain of failure in the same way that it is not naive about success, as may be the optimist. Vision of this kind differs fundamentally from the observation that seeks only to affirm a prejudice or a precious value.

A newspaper cartoon regarding the difference is called to mind here, where three fellows are staring at a glass of water. They state, in sequence, "As a pessimist, I say the glass is half empty." Then, "As an optimist, I say the glass is half full." And finally, "As an optometrist, I say what's the difference?" With the exception of not recognizing that there are clear differences in attitudes and expectations between the pessimist and the optimist, skepticism looks at the world more like the optometrist. We see what there is to see, and only then consider the odds of a value outcome, bad or good. This kind of vision ideally is more clear than any value position that stems from a desire to have one's feelings or desires about the world evidenced in some external manner. We are uniquely capable of thinking our own future, of thinking ahead, hence both the anxiety and aspiration actually involved in doing so. It is quite human to have trepidations about that which has not yet empirically or historically occurred. We know from what indeed *has* already occurred that a thing might not turn out at all as we had hoped or expected. We might think this ability to know and to not know simultaneously is a kind of curse on humanity,

> But we are creatures who have been endowed by nature itself with the capacity to take up a bold and possibly perilous distance in relation to our own natural being. By virtue of this endowment we are "exposed" in a certain way. We are, in particular, exposed to an awareness of our own future. For a human being is the creature who can think the future and who seeks to know how things will turn out in advance. But this distinguishing characteristic of human beings is also what makes them dangerous to themselves. (Gadamer 1996:85)

The sense that in order to know the future—an empirical impossibility by definition—means that we spend inordinate amounts of energy and time trying to control outcomes both in our personal lives and in the lives of cultures, ironically poses this great threat to our ability to indeed have a future at all. Predictability is one of the major motives for the rationalization processes outlined at the beginning of this book, and to which many of the routines and bureaucratic rituals we have recently adopted in our social and institutional organization tend. It is not enough to say, in a rather hackneyed way, that the "world is uncertain," or that we live in "uncertain times." Such phrases have little meaning as they are trivially true due to the ambiguity of mortal existence and the anxieties that emanate therefrom. It is our time itself that is uncertain—how human beings experience time and the world is apparently not as any other animals. We are divorced from our original biological templates and instincts by millions of years of cultural evolution, language, and unique community. We do not know the timing of our personal demise even while we are all too aware that at some time we will die. It is more than a trivially true circumstance that we may well have projected this odd combination of ultimate knowledge and ignorance onto the world at large. Whether we practice strictly rational and hardheaded science or we engage in a variety of other narratives that depart from the empirical—from statistical probability to faith, for example—we are faced with the same question. We cannot exactly predict what we also most wish not to know. The gravest threat to our humanity is by trying to know the very knowledge that the mythic Prometheus hid from us. The hiding of the knowledge of the moment of our own deaths makes all of what is human possible. To predict this moment with any aplomb would ironically push us to become something other than human—a cybernetic organism, perhaps, which would be relatively immortal and not subject to the purely organic breakdown or sudden fragility that we experience with our physical beings as human. Indeed, we live today in the period where the first signs of the next fundamental step in human evolution are taking place, from artificial intelligence to computer implants in our bodies. Perhaps we do long so strenuously for life itself that we would willingly abandon our human guise and take up a new form of consciousness. However this may be, it is clear that such a quest, for the time being, would involve the entirety of our being, emotional and rational, and be driven by both skepticism and pessimism concerning our current chances of survival as "merely" human.

Perhaps this is also why there has been, following the end of the Second World War, and the exposition of the horrors of the Holocaust and the subsequent cynical rationalizations offered for it at Nuremberg, that we long for examples of beings who have overcome their version of the existential anxiety and moved on. The fetish of high technology is one outcome of the drive to become more than we are—to become all the more the "prosthetic gods," as Freud famously and sardonically said of us. The idea that other imagined beings who hail from distant star systems indeed must have such technology and thus must be fundamentally different in their attitudes and outlooks on life and nature is also appealing to us. Yet, in the absence of public empirical evidence, we are left with pure anxiety and pure aspiration, as well as with the sense that the truth is not truly enlightening at all but somehow degrading:

> It is telling that emotions can run so high on a matter about which we really know so little. This is especially true of the more recent flurry of alien abduction reports. After all, if true, either hypothesis—invasion by sexually manipulative extraterrestrials or an epidemic of hallucinations—teaches us something we certainly ought to know about. Maybe the reason for strong feelings is that both alternatives have such unpleasant implications. (Sagan 1996:94)

These kinds of alternatives abound in a society that seeks to know with more certainty the outcomes of actions in the present, or vindicate memories of events that, either real or imagined—and there is in truth a mixture of both in every human memory—that occurred to us in the past. That we often focus on situations where the range of possible explanations is rather bleak does not automatically suggest pessimism about human affairs and our ability to guide them to viable fruition. It might be said that we are showing a kind of concernful being in our stance that sets out a suite of possible explications as warnings, giving us the sense that we need to be aware, or even beware, of one of the ways in which we live our lives in the present. It is the same for us with much more profound problems than even the idea that our anxieties are producing pathological "waking dreams" or our aspirations are producing visions of more advanced beings that come equally to save us from ourselves. The sense that history, and especially but not exclusively, recent history, is increasingly bereft of examples of "the good" in human affairs is perhaps the most stentorian call to pessimism. It does not seem to matter that the new metaphysics or the old both contain a more or less equal dose of light and dark:

> The atheist and the deist are arguing within similar frameworks: We know the standards, and we know what happens to people. And they can thus score points against each other. And when we look at the most horrifying sides of natures and history, it is the atheist who tends to score. For the Christian, these arguments of negative theodicy, a condemnation of any God who might claim to exist, are deeply disturbing, as is indeed, any tragic event seen up close: the death of a loved one, for example. But they realize that that are helpless to argue against these accusations. To do so, one would have to know, that means to be able to exhibit or demonstrate things we will never know. The case for the defense depends on there being more to human fate than we can exhibit as undeniable in history: that these people died in the earthquake, and those in gas chambers, and no-one came to rescue them. Christians can only reply to the accusations with hope. (Taylor 2007:389)

The situation may indeed be both better and still worse than is imagined here. We also know that history is rewritten, often with the whitewash of political convenience fashionable to this or that age. Holocaust deniers will only grow in number, for instance, after the last survivor of the events is dead. When mortal memory retreats in the face of the ongoingness of history, the lived memory of what will become history changes. The science of history, and that of archaeology, cannot always ameliorate this kind of change, as both are also functions of their social context, the paradigms of the day, and human hopes, fear, and imagination. This is indeed a sobering thought, I think more so than the sense that one is bereft of entities that can reach into the flow of human history and arrest events as if human relations were a sea that could be parted *deus ex machina* at any time. Perhaps we are so well aware of this lack that we have become more and more unscrupulous regarding our fellow human beings. Some of us may be certain that divine judgment was given to those tried at Nuremberg, and many thousands more besides, but we cannot be sure of this, and the modern mind is not likely to be empathetic to this vision quest, in part no doubt because part of us wishes to perpetrate our own petty version of such ultimate events in our own lives. The ethics demanded by optimism are apparently just as unrealistic as those demanded by the claimed realm of a transcendental being. The ethics of pessimism in turn claim to make no promises to us given the dead weight of history seen through its dark glass.

Yet the scene is also better than all of this. There are plenty of bright and inspiring events even in recent human history, though they tend to occur at a more individuated level, and if they occur structurally, they are slow in coming and sometimes diffuse in their effects. The sudden radicality of violence can only be met by the gradual recompense of care and compassion. The "good," as we have constructed it, does not erupt like the bad. The contexts where something is valued as "good" that is sudden and seemingly spontaneous are either those of the neighbor figure on the profound side, or those that involve some athletic or technical prowess—like a "great play" or "great shot" in a sporting event—on that trivial. Even so, these kinds of historic moments exist side by side the great tragedies, giving perspective to our more shadowy proclivities. As well, we are certainly now well beyond the point in our modern discourse where we see the effects of an anonymous nature as bad or good in themselves. They may be dangerous for us as human beings, but they are not maleficent. Any resonance of anthropomorphism—or projection of human desire and character into nature—aids only pessimism, and sabotages skepticism, for it suggests that what is fundamentally nonhuman and aloof to human concerns is "out to get us" in some bizarre manner. Finally, the ability we have to rewrite history as we live within its inertia also can produce more charitable interpretations of the past. Denial of evil can itself be seen as evil, but we also know that even at times where the negative extremes are most present in our consciousness—indeed, it is a living part of what it means to be human, and thus cannot be truly denied—there is resistance to it, and attempts to balance it with other, more humane forces.

So the contiguity of the rewriting of history for better or worse, the rational understanding of an impersonal cosmos, and the recognition of the good in the mundane face to face or even its more entertaining function in the technical, all serve to cast our current situation in a more realistic spectrum of possibility. Taylor is more on the mark when he suggests that the individual can be a vehicle for one of the main characteristics of the sacred in human history:

> Modern individualism, as a moral idea, doesn't mean ceasing to belong at all—that's the individualism of anomie and break-down—but imagining oneself as belonging to ever wider and more impersonal entities:

the state, the movement, the community of humankind.
(ibid:211)

Although not as intimate as those found in traditional societies, these new forms of belonging carry within them the seeds of perspective and the promise of overcoming our parochiality. We often hear this kind of hope echoed when science fiction fans or authors, or eminent scientists themselves, speak of the effect of possible future extraterrestrial contact. The "childhood" of the human race would certainly be over in this one moment, but there are plenty of things native to earth and its cultures that are available for us to gain a greater maturity of being.

The problem remains for us to both see and be seen by these opportunities. When faced with crises that are recognizable, their very ability to be seen and perhaps partially comprehended signals that they are already arrived, and there is no other time than the moment in which to comprehend them. Certainly this is how many writers and witnesses describe the coming of Nazism, amongst other dangerous and criminal social movements, and although this may be in part a rationalization to assuage our bad conscience for not acting "in time"—which in these situations always feels like "ahead of time"—or for excusing silent complicity, we are also aware that many things in fact do takes us unawares. It is a little contrary for us to follow the old adage "expect the unexpected." The events that construct crises can also be given hyperbolic power, much like their own subaltern versions of the myth of the state, in order to foster the comfortable pessimism that says *had we known, we could not have done anything anyway*. This kind of situation has its own fascism to it, and speaking of it, Arendt suggests that:

> All this was real enough as it took place in public; there was nothing secret or mysterious about it. And still,

> it was by no means visible to all, nor was it at all easy to perceive it; for, until the very moment when catastrophe overtook everything and everybody, it was covered up not by realities but by the highly efficient talk and double-talk of nearly all official representatives who, without interruption and in many ingenious variations, explained away the unpleasant fact and justified concerns. (Arendt 1968:viii)

There is a cycle of impending crisis and the amelioration of our perception of it by both our elected and unelected "representatives." The fraudulent motives for the invasion of Iraq, as well as the fraudulent exchange of capital that led to the current economic woes of much of the world, are recent versions of this cycle. In any hierarchical society where certain status groups maintain their status by constant aggrandizement, there will be the reality of charade and the keeping up of appearances that not only is all well but that those who are in charge know what they are doing and can be trusted to act on our behalf. We have already seen the response to this idea by Weber and others. Orwell's *1984* was prescient of a kind of fascism that makes the visible invisible and controls the vision of all who seek to see the world as it is. We are not yet living in such a total society. Like all ultimate metaphors, dystopias and utopias both are ideal types that likely cannot exist, at least not for long, in the human condition. Yet it is important to note that the pessimism of the dystopic situation does not seem to be as unrealistic as the Eden-like metaphors of the utopia. It may well be that it is more convenient for those who are charged with maintaining the social order to overemphasize crisis. Call a person's or a culture's security into doubt, as was done after the 2001 attacks on the United States, and those people are more willing to give over their power of decision and even reflective thought to those who sound the alarm. The alert to insecurity must be coupled with the promise of future security, or the rehabilitation of our comfort zones, in order for the ulterior motive of power and it's potentially carte blanche abuse to come to fruition. Then the threat to security must be "made good" in two ways. First, it must be maintained as a viable belief by crisis-oriented action—the crisis itself must be extended and reaffirmed in our minds. Second, we must be delivered from the crisis by the intervention of the forces acting on behalf of those who alerted us to it. All religious and political revolutions have this structure. Whether one is a messiah or a more earthly leader matters not. All charismatic authority proclaims itself as seer. The new would-be order has a clearer vision of what is to come, and whatever version of the apocalypse is proclaimed, and it is in the service of the ordination of the new regime that it is maintained over at least a plausible period of time. There are vested interests in dragging the current round of conflict out in the Middle East, and not merely on the side of investment capital, arms sales, and infrastructure and oil agreements. The local sides, too, given their fractious factions, need war, not peace, to further their own political and quasi-religious ambitions. On this side, the expense is paid by the local people, especially women, who by the happenstance of birth live in this region, and by ourselves, the rest of the West who works and does not own, whose children may appear to voluntarily join professional militaries—it is well known sociologically that almost all recruits are from the economic margins of capital in countries where mandatory military service is not required—and those who have to live with the anxiety of waiting for their potential return.

We are aware of this, in the manner Arendt suggested. Yet, at the same time, we are confronted with situations and forces which require us to become aware of these things in another way. This new form that is peddled by interest groups—perhaps because even those who appear powerful have doubts that need to be assuaged and ethical compunctions that exhort them to at least give the appearance of "doing something" rather than giving up—has an inchoate form. It is more like a series of disconnected feelings rather than even a mood:

> Everyone senses that something has changed. Often this is experienced as a loss, break-up. A majority of Americans believe that communities are eroding, families, neighbourhoods, even the polity; they sense that people are less willing to participate, to do their bit; and they are less trusting of others. Scholars do not necessarily agree with this assessment, but the perception itself is an important fact about today's society. No doubt there are analogous perceptions widespread in other Western societies. (Taylor 2007:473)

As a professor of sociology who also teaches introductory classes, I am very well aware that the data of the social sciences is hardly a part of contemporary life. It does not impinge either on the propaganda of state and corporate media or on the casual observations of the direct experience of individuals. Yet *perception* is an ambiguous word. There is no real way to judge a perception "in itself." Where do these observations and their individuated hypotheses come from? How are they massaged and manipulated by institutions, if they are noticed at all? And what does it mean to hold a nonscientific understanding of society and human relations? Usually, our individual experiences lead us into comfortable corners. We end up seeing what we want to see. Not that this in itself is necessarily a cause of pessimism or cynicism. It may be that we need this space to embark from ourselves and thence to return to ourselves transformed. There is no better beginning than one that can at least know a portion of itself as its own language. We are, sometimes uncomfortably and nervously, nevertheless at home in our own beings. Indeed, there is no other place to begin, even for the scientist. But once begun, the journey into the world as it is sees our vision depart radically from not only the parochial world of individual experience but also its models of the world, filled with desire and attempts at wish fulfillment, as well as perhaps denial of dangerous situations, both to self and society, and as we have seen, hyperbolic inflation of artificial crises. The mixture of sources of optimism and pessimism crowd in on our ability to step back and exercise a reflective skepticism. When we encounter, scientifically or otherwise, simple human contexts that make us feel pain or bad conscience, we quite expect that the next time we encounter something that makes us feel good, or assuages our conscience, we will latch on. What has transpired in the meantime is the process by which pessimism is grounded as a reality—because we feel so badly and those feelings are real—as well as the experiential fact that we can recover from such bad feelings. Thus, the world seems in a constant smaller-than-life cycle of dark and light. The worlds of which we remain unaware remain in shadows, potentially ambiguous in their loyalty to the good or to the bad. Having a moral tradition that emphasizes the duality of nature as either good or evil semiconsciously reaffirms this experiential interpretation of social reality. That this nature is part of who we are and how we have always been is the stock in trade rhetoric of any morality, and it is as false a judgment on the world as it is as any moral judgment has ever been. We have already seen that it is the ethical endeavor that places us within the reality of the human world, and morality merely charts a set of principles derived and then abstracted from it. Indeed, one may go to great lengths to suggest that, in spite of the presence of what has been called evil in the world, we are more alert to the idea of evil itself in our lives. This does not necessarily mean we act to prevent it, nor even that we cease our compounding of it by ignoring it—or yet further, enjoying it—when it has occurred or continues to occur. It does means, however, that what we take to be evil today is a sign that we know more about the good than did our ancestors:

> The shift is in a recognizably consistent direction, which most of us would judge as an improvement. Even Adolf Hitler, widely regarded as pushing the envelope of evil into uncharted territory, would not have stood out in the time of Caligula or Genghis Khan. Hitler no doubt killed more people than Genghis, but he had twentieth-century technology at his disposal. And did even Hitler gain his greatest *pleasure*, as Genghis avowedly did, from seeing his victims' "near and dear bathed in tears"? We judge Hitler's degree of evil by the standards of today, and the moral *Zeitgeist* has moved on since Caligula's time, just as technology has. Hitler seems especially evil only by the more benign standards of our time. (Dawkins 2006:268–69)

An odd example, perhaps, and we moderns would certainly not want to hang our collective ethical hats on such a figure. Yet it is reasonable, and less pessimistic, to view certain histories as containing the ability to be morally outraged at acts of injustice, which at least appear through the lens of that same history either as more widespread in the past, or, as is more likely, that the official accounts that we do have of "history" as it may be include only the rationalizations of violence. That a "god was on their side" was certain for the victors. Aside from the enlightenment, which tended to downplay the moral diversity of earlier ages given its own sense of superiority in this regard, it is fair to suggest that people today are a little more aware that violence and injustice inflicted on their fellows just because one can do so through strength or through greed, ressentiment, lust, or avarice of other kinds is, in principle at least, immoral. It is more technologically convenient today to kill more people, but it appears that it is less politically or morally convenient to do so.

Needless to say, those kinds of perhaps growing inconveniences have not stopped us. The twentieth century is by far the bloodiest century known to humankind. This fact alone spurs the pessimist to advantage. Yet, for every violence, there is much more likely to be resistance, as not only are we linked in a global village more intimately than ever before but through international media, which, no matter how censored and controlled by elites, does report injustice both at home and abroad. No doubt such reportage is fashionable to the political and lifestyle conveniences of our social and public realities. We have not yet pushed ourselves to adopt environmentally sound energy sources, for example, or disarmed ourselves of offensive weapons systems. We are not merely pessimistic about such changes occurring quickly, masking this under the guise of skepticism; we are also cynical in our attitude toward others, as we imagine them to be entirely maleficent in their desires. Perhaps we see ourselves too clearly in the eyes of the other, and this makes us yet more uncomfortable. The idea that we must always protect ourselves and our lifestyle from the world at large is writ small in the competition capital fosters between citizens of developed nation-states. Charity and philanthropy are fine, but modest structural change in even our tax systems seems at present beyond our will.

We do not, in taking this line, see the entire picture. Most people want such changes and we simply do not know how to go about putting them in place. Most of us are not represented by elite interests and we do not expect to be. *After all,* we say to ourselves, *why would others care for us when we, given the same position, might act as they do?* Vowing ethical superiority is usually the language of the optimist. It is neither reflective nor skeptical enough. When asked, most people are generous if they know to whom and where there generosity flows. Yes, there are some others whom we disdain, and we often practice a "blaming the victim" rhetoric toward them. We may be on the cusp of awareness that there are few completely innocent situations, where our fellows and ourselves have been completely duped and have been in utter ignorance of the effects of our actions. A genealogy of each such context requires ethical reflection, skepticism, and critique. To not dive in too immediately with either charity or chastisement could be seen as the incipient light of such a process. Furthermore, when opportunities arise to become aware of injustice and to react with less pessimism, such are commodified and sold to us very much like any other object or political cause, and our motives become ambiguous:

> ... we sense immediately how fragile is this motivation. It makes our philanthropy vulnerable to the shifting fashion of media attention, and the various modes of feel-good hype. We throw ourselves into the cause of the month, raise funds for this famine, petition the government to intervene in that grisly civil war, and then forget all about it next month, when it drops off the CNN screen. A solidarity ultimately driven by the giver's own sense of moral superiority is a whimsical and fickle thing. We are far in fact from the universality and unconditionality which our moral outlook prescribes. (Taylor 2007:696)

So it is not that we are, by our cultural senses and our moral proclivities, unendingly inattentive to injustice, even that of which we are the perpetrators, but rather that we can only abide concern for the other if it is presented as something the strong must do for the weak. *Ressentiment* is no doubt fostered by such a stance, which is in fact not only unethical but existentially false, as those now strong can be rendered impotent at any moment by the vagaries of the human condition. In fact, our fashionable concern for others suggests that we are trying to deny our own existential situation, not only with regard to others, but more precisely, with regard to anyone who shows us that we too are as they are, weak and fragile, passing and mortal, humanly needful.

These kinds of existential realities are not only occluded by a personal sense that one desires not to think of them as part of the day-to-day routines of life, let alone circumstances that can interrupt our more precious dreams of intimacy and community and our more base—yet still necessary— aspirations of success and vocational fulfillment, but by larger and more contrived forces. Whatever the institutional milieu, history is written in the hand of organizations that, because they seem to live on after those who had populated them at any one point in time are dead, appear to us as larger than life itself. It does not matter if they themselves undergo momentous changes, as they have done so in the past century: "Politically speaking, it was the decline and downfall of the nation state; socially, it was the transformation of a class system into a mass society; and spiritually it was the rise of nihilism, which for a long time had been a concern of the few but now, suddenly, had become a mass phenomenon." (Arendt 1968 228–89)

These kinds of shifts in the structure of larger-than-life social realities can easily give us the impression as individuals that not only do we not matter much in the grand scheme of things but, worse still, that we are both the objects of the historical process and subject solely to its currents and whims. This is not the same thing as the idea, suggested above by Gadamer, that we are mainly subject to the inertia of history as ideas and as the structures of human consciousness. Nihilism, a particularly fatalistic version of pessimism and cynicism combined, is the result only if we comprehend history as an anonymous force with no human interest, and that we, in the face of such a force, are helpless to become humane and concernful beings who do, even if in a smaller way, rewrite history as we live on within it.

Skepticism avoids this pitfall by balancing what actually occurs in social reality—institutions and organizations do change, individuals both good and bad come and go, change is slow but apparent, and sometimes changes for the better happen as suddenly as shifts for the worse—with the emotional yet empirically definable events of human hopes and fears. We know by now, after the horrors of the twentieth century and without needing to imagine what worse that may lie over the horizon, that knowledge in the modern sense will not be enough for us to survive and flourish. What the enlightenment gave us in terms of critique, reflection, and sense of human destiny unfettered by the limits of religious fate seems lacking. Or it may be that we are simply unpracticed, apprentices to a new metaphysics that has yet to be mastered, students of a new humanity that has yet to be learned. Either way, what we have been doing

> ... isn't enough. That is, I think humanity is more likely to go down this semi-catastrophic road. It might become an epidemic that one cannot control, that one cannot predict. Anything at all could make it so that our angst brings humanity to a halt. If angst, as it were, threatens everyone, then perhaps there is hope that people will come to an understanding of some sensible conception of transcendence—perhaps people will begin to ask themselves why we are born without being asked, why we die without being asked, and so on. (Gadamer 2004:142)

Not only does the fact remain that to be human, the concept of the sacred cannot be eschewed, but the idea that our mortality really means something outside of itself must be tended to in some manner. "Transcendence" here does not necessarily point to the history of religion as we have known it in Western consciousness but to the very same event that caused the just aforementioned discomfort of institutions and politics living longer than human beings.

We, while alive, make and remake these realities. They are other guises of our collective thought and action. They are still our own, in other words, and do not live on without us, when we begin to think of just what it means to be part of a community and a society. To become humane one must not lose sight of the fact that what we are as individuals not merely "affects" others, as we tell our children as a fundamental part of the socialization process and becoming human, but is in fact created by the interaction and relations with others. Oneself thought of as another might see us is a way of understanding the ethics of human community.

So the idea of hope, just as much a feeling or mood as it might be something one reflects upon or calculates is not necessarily linked to a religious or even scientific concept of a life beyond this life. It might simply mean "confidence in life, in the life-struggle for our own survival." (Grondin 2003:329), for instance. To be hopeful is also a more sincere situation: "The pessimist is disingenuous because he is trying to trick himself with his own grumbling. Precisely while acting the pessimist, he secretly hopes that everything will not turn out as bad as he fears." (ibid.) The sense that we also live with the anxiety of having to imagine not living, that is, the unknowingness that our own demise presents to ourselves, no doubt colors sharply the undertaking of encountering with sincerity the other, for this encounter, as we have seen, must necessarily hasten the rehearsal of a kind of death of our previously living selves within the life course: "We are characterized by the fact that we are not simply identical with a kind of 'life' which reproduces itself, but rather that each and every one of us, as an individual, must die their own death." (Gadamer 1996:150) This knowledge of the one thing that cannot be truly known to us also suggests that knowledge itself, though born of curiosity, wonder, and awe, cannot dispel, once known, any of these things. So hope is also the effort to become knowledgeable, the will to know.

The knowledge that the religious life presents to us goes no farther than that of other forms to this regard. Science, too, presents itself as ultimately a hopeful vocation. Whatever the uses to which our knowledge is put in the meanwhile, the scientific understanding of the cosmos loses none of its awe. This process of making sacred the idea that human beings are those local intelligences that can know the universe in an ordered manner, and that such an order includes ourselves, however nominally, cannot provoke disdain or pessimism, no matter if it reduces our vanity to its proper place. It also reminds us that we are manifestly *not* the focus or center of the nature of being, though we must remain the center of our own existence. The anonymity of cosmic nature and the seeming insignificance of our place within it belie the sometimes tragic outcomes of our deliberations on both self *and* world.

> But nevertheless there is something important here. A too benign picture of the human condition leaves something crucial out, something that matters to us. There is a dark side to creation... along with joy, there is massive innocent suffering and then on top of this, the suffering is denied, the story of the victims is distorted, eventually forgotten, never rectified or compensated. Along with communion, there is division, alienation, spite, mutual forgetfulness, never reconciled and brought together again.... Even where a voice of faith wants to deny that this is the last word, we cannot set aside the fact that this is what we live, that we regularly experience this as ultimate. All great religious recognize this, and place their hopes in a beyond which simply doesn't deny this, which takes its reality seriously. (Taylor 2007:319)

For some, this potential overcoming of one life through another, more noble and yet less human than our own, is not serious enough. Action within the world is the order of the day. Each of us becomes then a kind of vehicle for the local version of a "liberation theology" that says that what human knowledge is for is to overcome suffering in this very human life and for all humans. This also means being able to experience the risk of our serial living deaths in the face of the *other*, as something to do with hope, and not to be pessimistic about our survival simply because we note with nostalgia that our own individual guises of self come and go as we live on. The skeptical understanding recognizes the reality of not merely human suffering, as epic as this is, but also the reality that otherness presents the ultimate challenge to our sense of what human consciousness can or even should be. Yet it does not turn aside from knowing either that suffering or that challenge:

> Here lies my own deepest hope, or perhaps I should say, dream: that from the shared inheritance which is gradually being built up for us from all the different human cultures across the globe we might eventually learn how to recognize our needs and address our difficulties through becoming explicitly conscious of them. (Gadamer 1996:78)

The imposing diversity that presents the most challenging fact of being human and attempting to know and share a common humanity indeed is the very vehicle for such a knowledge. It cannot be otherwise, as what we ourselves have been in our own individual lives ultimately becomes other to us. That this can connote pessimism is undeniable, but this manner of experiencing the world as change is too casual and shallow. The pessimist, quite simply, gives up too soon in giving into the idea that change means loss, above all. Rather, whatever must be sacrificed to live on can be seen as growth, maturing of being, experience and knowledge anew. We do, rather contrarily, experience our own deaths in this way, and this can give us the balance of hope and reality that skepticism is characterized by. In experiencing this strange contiguity of both life and death—the one ongoing because the other has stepped in and pushed it along, as it were—we are always close to recovering sincere awe at the fact of our own existence. Such a wonder is not vanity. It is the recognizance that we are as unlikely a life form as we are unlike any other form of life. We err only in thinking that we must conserve this in the face of new life. Whether of our past selves or of others who have changed, and ultimately, others who have finally passed on, we desire to extend what we have known into what will be known in the future. This is not always possible, of course, but to wish it to be so is not the desire of vanity or childishness:

> It is rather an irrepressible need of human nature not only to preserve the character of the dead person, which has been transformed through permanent separation, but to reconstruct it in its productive and positive form. It is changed into an ideal and, as an ideal, becomes itself unchangeable. It is difficult to say what is really taking place in this process whereby, in the final separation from someone, we come to experience their presence in a different way. (Gadamer 1996:67)

This need, and its effects, is reflective of the will to life itself. The reality of living joins with the hope of what is to be lived. The disposition that results is neither pessimistic nor optimistic but rather is the cautious and experienced stance of the skeptic, who knows, if anything, that human knowledge is born of transformation and borne on the transformative powers of the historical process. It is this process that makes mortal knowledge itself immortal to us, and thus finally overcomes its own finitude.

Modesty and Humility

THE TANDEM of terms that will occupy us for the final chapter of this journey is the most difficult to differentiate. We often use modesty and humility in the same situations, for the same contexts or feelings. Why even attempt to distinguish them? Put simply, modesty is something that more often than not is placed upon us from within. Although dress codes, sexual diplomacies, and an injunction against braggadocio may appear to be an imposition of an external authority, a wider society or sense of etiquette, perhaps, to be modest is only reconciled when we ourselves decide it is a good thing for us, and furthermore I will argue, eventually a good in itself. In fact, it is this very reconciliation that allows what may be a power over us to be resisted, transformed, and made into a part of our ethical beings. The forced conformity of social roles or mores and norms indeed becomes modest only when we rebuild them as something for us and not something ranged against us, suppressing our desires or our personalities.

It is very much otherwise with the case of humility. Within this word, we can already see its disconcerting relatives; humiliation and being humbled. In a word, humility never departs from its external and coercive source. It overcomes us rather than we overcoming it, as is the case with what becomes modesty. Humility is an attitude not merely of deference to a norm or an edict, but a submission to an order, social, personal, or even divine. One is humbled against one's will in humility, and often, through humiliation, the will of the other as coercive and demanding gets the better of us, rendering us impotent and out of touch with the reality of our singular beings, and alienated from the very community in which we seek succor. Ironically, it is sometimes this very community that forces us to conformity. If this is recognized, and if we feel the strain to be too much of an imposition not merely on our own sense of self-worth and direction, but on general human freedom, we must part ways with such a group. We are aware that this kind of farewell occurs daily, and, as we have discussed above, is in fact necessary at certain points of life in order to grow into the beings we imagine ourselves to eventually be. From the most extreme personal cases—the abused spouse in a domestic situation who feels a compulsion not to leave, or children whose lack of autonomy forces them to stay put— to the extremities of wider historical events—the forced labor and murder of millions through genocide—humility is what is sought, not by the victim or the oppressed as a gauge of morality and sense of mortal fragility, but by the perpetrator, as a gauge of loyalty and obedience.

Let me give a somewhat bizarre series of related examples of the difference. For three years or so, I once studied sociologically the subculture of people who enjoy submitting themselves to sexual theaters of discipline and correction, as well as those who erotically enjoyed meting these out. The former were more masochistic in their tendencies and gratifications, the latter, sadistic. The old joke about the true sadist who refuses to beat the masochist of course comes to mind here. In my travels in and around these fellow humans I was struck with their sense of ethical rationalization. The sadists performed a service for the masochists, giving them what they desired in a more or less safe and consenting manner. The masochist was proud of his or her ability to trust and give various serious forms of power to another, many of whom were relative strangers. Of course, all of these folks were adults, which brings me to the first problem. Humility, amongst these people, was a theatrical prop as well as being something to be desired or demanded. In itself, it was not a moral virtue. Modesty, in the old-fashioned sense of prudery and shame was nowhere to be found, yet in our sense, the pleasures of the mortification of the flesh and the sometimes confessed atonement for whatever "sins" one might have imagined committing in the past or even in the future, was present in abundance. Here, modesty took on the transformative character of something to be displayed from within. The rhetoric of these theaters of mock cruelty mocked precisely humility and the inauthentic modesty of fascist social contexts such as boarding schools and prisons. Through this mockery and nostalgia, a truer accounting of one's desires and lusts appeared, as well as an exposition of the hypocritical lust that had clothed the objects of desire from an early age. This brings me back to my point about the problem: Much of this subculture pretends that one or another of its actors—adult persons playing roles in order to fulfill desire—in fact portray themselves as children or adolescents.

What is going on here? Well, a number of things, not all comforting. First, given that most of us experience power at first through the often coercive movement of primary socialization, and that we are dependent upon those who appear to be powerful for our very means of survival, the sense that trust is first of all thrust upon us as a necessity of accepting the situation of youthful human life, rather than as a dialogue between relative equals, lends an immediacy to the idea that "power over" makes one at least theatrically regress into a childhood scene. Second, if this occurs as part of an erotic or sensual stimulation then there is present the idea that one becomes most desirable as an object of coercion. That is, we are all the sexier the more submissive and masochistic we appear to be. That these persons can always find dominant others to play the roles of parents, teachers, or other potential authoritarians speaks ill not only about our general manner of indoctrinating children into our society, but that some of us gain pleasure from inflicting the repetition of this process. The ability to wield various ritual forms of power over others is addicting in this way. We presume that those who wish to be dominated are also subject to the needful repetition of the dominance. That it is considered playful by insiders perhaps tells us only part of the story. *Why play like this?* is a query to which members of such subcultures respond to only with the relativism of all in-groups. They say something like, *This is our kink and we like it, and nothing more needs to be said about it*. This may be so for the indulgent adult, even if the settings provide grist for the psychiatric mills. But can the same deadpan response suffice for the rest of us more generally, who also practice versions of these melodramas in our own homes, schools, and elsewhere with the social sanction that this is not only what is necessary to train children to become adults but that these normative power relations are also satisfying in some other manner. Given the social hierarchy, given that all of us have been dominated before we may become dominant, given that most of us do not dominate in the same total manner as we may have been subject to at least in our public life, there seems to be ample room for the taking of real pleasure, sexual, aesthetic, or otherwise, from the control of and authority over others, large or small.

It does not stop there, of course. The disciplinary sadomasochistic subculture, as with all sexual or erotic scenes and themes, is in full presence on the Internet. The theaters are obvious, if stilted, and one wonders what the younger audience of these kinds of arenas makes of them, especially if they undergo the less mock version in their own lives. We may worry about our children seeing "too much" of what we wish to deny ourselves, but none of this is illicit or pornographic. This word, which in casual use is often confused with *erotica*—which points up the possibility of another chapter, if this book were less serious than it hopes to be—technically means *sexual act without consent*—a crime in most regions of the world (though not within most cultures' ideas of marriage, ironically). Animals, corpses, assaults on adults, and, of course, our most pressing concern, children or minors, are included in the criminal category of sexual deviance. All other forms involve, sometimes quite literally, "paying your money and taking your chances." Many of us do, and there is no true crime in this. Yet identifying problems only in the areas where they are most transparent—child pornography, though relatively rare, is a burgeoning problem on the Internet—misses the wider point about just exactly why there is so much of this other stuff around anyway. The sociologist, as opposed to the criminologist, must ask a wider question. What is it about sexuality, power, and the aesthetics of dominance and submission (or other kinks) that is so popular and yet so taboo at the same time? The confusion between modesty and humility has, I think, something quite directly to do with it.

    Before exploring this point further, let me take another, yet more shadowy route for a few moments, and then attempt to bring us back to the theme of the chapter, and thence finally, to the implications of all of our discussions thus far. It is certainly ethically correct that we are concerned about the exploitation of children in a sexual manner, although we tend to narrowly focus on their actual sexual subjugation rather than on their forms paraded in fashion advertising, the abuse of children—perhaps with sexual connotation made indirect through sadism—in the home and in schools, and the unpaid labor children do for their communities and the institutions in which they find themselves ensconced. No journey through the darker recesses of the Internet will not come across a few images of patently underage "models" either startled or adorable—either way uncomfortably desirable for many. And if one has the audacity to follow the links, then yet more images, and other media, will inevitably appear. During my field study, I was surprised at the weight of our general socialization regarding these things. When an image of this sort appeared on my screen, I automatically closed my eyes, and winced, as if I had indeed witnessed a kind of "abomination of the desecration" writ small. I tried to condition myself not to do this, but only got so far with it. Indeed, I was relieved that my research was not criminological in nature, and I wondered about those who choose to engage in such work, necessary as it is.

Some years after this study was completed I read of a quirky juxtaposition in the *Los Angeles Times*, where a journalist who was investigating Internet pedophile reports came across a comment by the then Metro Toronto Police Department's head of their child pornography unit. The comment was in response to another journalist's question regarding patterns or things in common that potential or actual pedophiles exhibited. Aside from the "usual suspects" of hanging around kids in playgrounds and schools, and so forth, there was often found in the houses of the criminals a great deal of memorabilia and media associated with the famous science fiction saga *Star Trek*. My reaction was, simply, *huh?* at first, and then the Los Angeles journalist sought out this person in Toronto. The latter "explained" this contiguity of *Star Trek* and pedophilia by suggesting—after first demurring on whether or not he actually had a viable explanation—that the series exhibited a society in which there were no rules and where monsters controlled the universe. Aside from being a gross misrepresentation of these series and their at least average fan, there seemed to be no merit in the inspector's remarks. The facts remain, however. Police *do* find these artifacts of popular culture, and specifically to do with Star Trek in these odd and dismal contexts. I think there is more to this than coincidence, although one cannot abet the idea that *Star Trek*—very much a moral homiletic in much of its plot and scripts that takes us to the very opposite of the society the police inspector imagined—leads one in the direction or tacitly condones criminal acts of very much any kind, let alone pedophilia. Rather "science fiction" in general represents the conflicts and ideals of what we know to be the human condition, and gives them a fresh perspective that is often quasi-sociological both in scope and reflection. Indeed, it usually has little enough to do with science, and it is fiction only in that it presents an allegory of our own social reality; other humans are indeed alien enough for us most of the time, perhaps none more so than those who exploit children in these ways, for example. The interest in *Star Trek* in particular and the practicing of abhorrent behavior more likely comes from the sense that the series' norms are presented as being beyond the reach of present-day reality. Whether or not we desire the "technological communism" of *Star Trek* society is another issue entirely. We only have to recognize that what is being sanctioned is thinking outside of the box, very often in nascently radical ways. This new horizon of thinking promoted by the scripts of *Star Trek* certainly does not include pedophilia, but it does give us the sense that such thinking—that which ignores the norms of society at large, and that which questions the normal activities of others, their intents and their beliefs—is not only possible but desirable in itself. The rub here is that, indeed, such thinking *is* desirable, and, indeed, this point has been made over and over again throughout the history of thought, let alone the nominal context of the argument of this book.

Again, we are left with the ethical problem of where and when to draw the line on rejecting social norms as habitual or ritual forms of unthought. I have a suspicion, based on my own scientific experience with persons who act out of the norms in sometimes risky and intimate ways, that what the personality of the pedophile is finding a reaffirmation of in science fiction is that what they do is somehow allowable and is an expression of true freedom. The problem here is that freedom in its most authentic sense is had through the other's freedom, and we are aware that children do not possess the requisite cognitive apparatus, let alone knowledge of the problem of free will and social structure, to consent to becoming objects for the freedom of an adult. This is so in every case of our relationships with children, and is grotesquely highlighted in the case of sexual assault.

That modesty prevents us from carrying the implications of our will to the blind extremities of annulling the other as a human being, and that humility promotes us giving too much over to that very other, further our sense that they cannot be confused as ethical concepts. Rationalizations abound concerning the hypocrisy of care for children and their socially sanctioned coercion, but this is more a manifestation of a larger structure of consciousness than a tacit way of saying that we are all haters of children yet we are comfortable with limits other than the pedophile's. That we have not abolished cruelty toward even our own children speaks of this structure. It may even be in part an historical limit to our imaginations. Taylor provides a like, and also current, example:

> ... something of this understanding applied in the general consciousness also to other differentiations, even where there may not have been an explicit doctrine to this effect. Thus the stance to the poor had the sense it

> did partly because it was taken for granted that "the poor ye have always with you." More, this made sense, because the poor, while being succoured by the fortunate, were also an occasion of salvation of these latter. There was a complementarity here, alongside a difference of worth.... Within this way of understanding, it was unthinkable that one try actually to abolish poverty. (Taylor 2007:123)

Although we may deride the thinking of our ancestors as narrow and showing a lack of imagination for the humanly possible, or even the humanly ethical, it is clear that we have our own version of "the box" that we are so often exhorted to think outside of, whether that push comes from our social philosophers or our advertisers: "This is easy to forget, because once we are well installed in the modern social imaginary, it seems the only possible one, the only one which makes sense. After all, are we not all individuals? Do we not associate in society for our mutual benefit? How else to measure social life?" (ibid:168)

Similar to the kinds of assumptions we make about sharing meaning, belief, and values with others deemed like ourselves, the unquestionable standards of modern life come across as second nature. Sociological commentaries regarding "of course" statements—questions that when asked could only generate the response of "of course," or the like, on our parts—is germane here. Along with all of the apparently natural routines of day to day life, "what people do, or what one does," there are those beliefs that are unquestionable due more to the sense that we know almost nothing about them. The science that underlies our technology and the metaphysics that supports our science, for example, would fall into this category. Perhaps yet more distant from us are the ethical "of course" statements, those that have to do with justifying privilege and lack thereof, justice and injustice, and social hierarchies and authorities of diverse kinds and contexts. All of the unquestioned questions generate a sense of humility. It takes modesty on our parts to confront them as real issues, to admit that they are as arbitrary as some other culture's rules and beliefs. The reality of historical relativity to this regard also seems not to faze us:

> Pre-moderns could be as untroubled by the fact of systemic inequality between orders and peoples and religious groups, which were part of the order of things, as contemporary ultra-liberals can be untroubled by a capitalism which generates a destitute underclass, which is also seen as part of an order where the idle and undisciplined get their just desserts. (ibid:578)

The sense of the appropriateness of all things is, of course, constructed by a socialization through which children are taught more to conform than to question. It is simply more convenient this way, as all societies in all times and places have found, to reproduce what has been. To see the past as what must be is, of course, only the extreme form of understanding history as having not merely an inertia but an honorable weight, before which we must be humbled. It is striking that in being so, we actually lose our modesty, for it is only the arrogant and unthinking person who claims that their tradition alone is worth reproducing, in the face of all others. A modest society is one full of queries, curiosity about others, and the knowledge of not only the arbitrariness of birth but of the shared meaning constructed by human communities.

So much so are we inured to our own social locations that we carry them throughout our lives, even through changing fortunes and perhaps yet even shifting structures of larger social institutions:

> It is reasonable to assume that it is just as hard for rich people grown poor to believe in their poverty as it is for poor people turned rich to believe in their wealth; the

> former seemed carried away by a recklessness of which they are totally unaware, the latter seemed possessed by a stinginess which actually is nothing but the old ingrained fear of what the next day may bring. (Arendt 1968:179)

The force of our primary socialization does as much to make society a mystery as it does to clarify our role within it. We eventually see through the part about what is said to be "not allowed" to us as children, and many of us transgress these boundaries just to prove that our youthful suspicions were correct. Yes, there may be consequences, but the idea of disallowing this or that action (or even this or that thought) needs be a fragile one indeed. Society, as we know, requires our consent in its function. We conspire to construct our own limits and, more darkly, seek to do so for others as well. The idea of society as a mélange of secrets allows us to be more forgiving than we ought to be regarding the immodesty of those who calculate official or institutional mysteries. Secrecy has even, in the post-war period, become a hot commodity in the world of entertainment fiction, the well-known television series *The X-Files* is one example.

Of course, perhaps the charm of involving oneself in a conspiracy is that one can never know quite enough about it. Yet society itself is the most enveloping and immense conspiracy of all time, and indeed, we tend to not at all know enough about how it became that way and how it maintains itself over time. One would think that we, as those who live within society and make it what it is, would in fact be "in the know" about its deepest recesses, that "we the people" would be the experts, and not merely the social scientists, whose knowledge is also, at best, partial and, at times, not even impartial. But the sciences of humanity have their own worlds of mystery, to which the rest of us have unequal access. After all, one has to go to a university, perhaps earn graduate degrees to know what scientists of all stripes are talking about, even when they are talking about us. The stakes are much higher when in fact we *are* the objects of science, because we often lack the forum to object to it and its effects. Just as Weber said earlier, it is very risky handing over ultimate power to elites of any kind:

> Further, military, political and intelligence communities tend to value secrecy for its own sake. It's a way of silencing critics, and evading responsibility—for incompetence or worse. It generates an elite, a band of brothers in whom the national confidence can be reliably vested, unlike the great mass of citizenry on whose behalf the information is presumably made secret in the first place. With a few exceptions, secrecy is deeply incompatible with democracy and with science. (Sagan 1996:39)

Just as there is much that may be kept from us, with the template of all of our socializations for it to rest upon and be compared with, there are many other things to which we are exposed as children and adults that could be said to be just as risky to the practice of science and democracy in a modest society. Sagan (ibid:39), notes that we bombard our children with much violence in media without the leavening effect of either the often dire consequences accorded the acts of violence—the proverbial living and dying by the sword might easily be one of them—or the gentleness of humane relations. Passion sells better than compassion, and we therefore may learn to value the former more highly, when in fact it is the latter that is the true motive of humane society. Indeed, without such a balanced presentation of our condition, "None of us knows what effect he or she really has as our actions are integrated into a larger context." (Gadamer 2001:85)

It also seems that, often enough, few of us care to know. It is true to say that all of us have been those effected in terms of the manifestation of large-scale structural changes in the mode of production, technology, and competition over resources. These transitions, most of them gradual enough to effect only some of us some of the time, yet cumulative enough to leave entire societies transformed over the course of a couple of generations, continue at an excited pace today, especially in the so-called developing world. In spite of repeated admonitions over the post-war decades, we do not with foresight attempt to generally account for these changes by providing them with a meaningful history but as well give an accounting of their effects. Most current problems of this type have in fact been around for a while, and their presence has not gone unnoticed:

> Any effort, therefore, to further automatize work must take account not only of temporary technological unemployment but of the situation of those overly privatized ones who still suffer from the residual barriers of family, poverty, and hierarchy we have inherited from the era dependent on inner-direction. But surely we can think of better things for them than the factory as a refuge from home, just as we can think of better ways of giving poverty-stricken people security and good medical care than shutting them up in prison. (Riesman 1950:320)

All of this sounds quite familiar three generations onward, especially given the recent and persistent economic downturns and crises. Prisons are still burgeoning, medical care still absent for many, and an open factory is now more a refuge from unemployment itself rather than a mere escape from a home life also still in transition. The empirical effects of our decisions over time still bear the impressive mark of humility and humiliation, rather than the reflective impress of modesty and moderation. This immodest way of managing our society may be traced in part to its ideological roots, where notions of mythic history and fate played an important role. Not only in the United States, but in all societies and nations where the idea of America is both loved and hated—often at the same time and for different reasons, or even in the same place but by different sectors of these other cultures—these ideas percolate through versions of human consciousness quite different in their origins from our own. We do not yet fully know what effects this odd transmigration of ideas and feelings may have in the world, but we do understand what it means for our ability to cope with change here at home; we know that such ideas impinge on our ability to cautiously take stock of the direction of society. If one begins with the idea of deterministic design, one must feel both the need to fulfill it and thus also to be at least locally accountable for it:

> What the activism of the American Revolutionaries added to this was a view of history as the theatre in which this Design was to be progressively realized, and of their own society as the place where this realization was to be consummated—what Lincoln will later refer to as "the last best hope on earth." It was this notion of themselves fulfilling Divine purposes which, along with the Biblical culture of Protestant America, facilitated the analogy with ancient Israel that often recurs in American official rhetoric of the early days. (Taylor 2007:448)

And not merely in the early incarnations of the national tongue, as modern Israel figures just as prominently in our modern rhetoric, not merely as a strategic ally, but as a strategic analogy. What occurs to Israel in some sense also occurs to us. Hence it should come as no surprise that those who despise the very existence of the Jewish state should amplify their anger in our direction. We are also living in a promised land, by the druthers of manifest destiny. We also have the burden of conscience of stolen lands, whether it be Palestine or the North American continent as a whole. We might indeed imagine that over time and over there, as has occurred in our backyards, that what resistance there is left amongst the displaced will fade and eventually become muted, assimilated into the wider margins of capital such as poverty, reservations and lack of status. Once again, humility, being humbled and humiliated before a superior authority or force is active in our cultural imagination here. A modest society would not long put up with the burning of conscience that such events would promote in the reflective mind. Not that we need to rush headlong to "make up" for history. Such a thing is not in our power as living beings of the present. What can be done is to not repeat the actions for which we may be justifiably critiqued and from which have come justifiable concerns on the part of margins everywhere. In part, the lack of our ability to think about these topics transparently has come from the idea that each one of us is a mere part of a grander purpose and that living life largely means to be caught up in something larger than life. Various other institutional processes have aided this sense: "One democratizes the rights of genius in order to be relieved from the personal task of education and need of education." (Nietzsche 2004:35 [1872]). Indeed, one cannot replace such a singular need and task with a process that is aimed at the more than one. In doing so, we end up with a kind of society that can remain viable only in its ability to avoid thinking about such issues as the relationship between mytho-poetic notions and mythically pathetic social realities.

It is not that we are incapable of thought of this kind — quite the contrary. It is more that such thinking disturbs the routine function of society and upbraids our immodesty at the same time. It is not that we relate to one another so much as passive objects and merely use each other as means to our ends, "The point is that, over and above the socialization of consumptive preferences and the exchange of consumptive shoptalk by the consumers' union, the membership is engaged in *consuming itself*. That is, people themselves, friendships, are viewed as the greatest of all consumables; the peer-group is itself a main object of consumption, its own main competition in taste." (Riesman 1950:82; italics in the original) The modest person cannot be self-consumed and would not be a desirable object to consume for others. However, we would readily consume those who exhibit humility, especially when exhibited before us in some kind of submissive posture—so much so, that this is, as already discussed above, a well-known erotic fetish. With humility, we are not led to ask the reflective question of whether we view others as ends in themselves or whether we use others as means to our own ends. The humble and humiliated other is automatically a means to an end, and we can easily place ourselves in the superior position as there are always desires in our own lives that take on the form of a task at hand, something to be ventured and completed. The modest other just as immediately gives us pause, forcing us to retreat in the face of both the resistance that modesty brings to the face-to-face abilities of self-consumption, but also because in maintaining modesty, we do not presume to be anything at all to the other, either a means or an end.

If the personal is indeed also the political and, of course, the other way around, it is crucial that we attain a sense of the differentiation of the modest and the humble. False humility is difficult to manufacture, however, while false modesty appears to be everywhere at once. Even in the subculture of the sadist and the masochist the humility shown by true adherents, and not merely professional actors, is real enough, and the lusty overtures of dominance equally so. Yet modesty, because it is reflective and resistant, is oddly fragile in the face of its contrived emulation. The politics of modesty are such that modesty can become consumed in a new way. The way in which it falters in the public sphere is the same manner in which it can be used to as a means in the private. In a word, modesty is also an attitude we take up toward ourselves, and thus it can be turned to the use of making ourselves into something we are not for the purposes of using an *other* as a means to our ends. All those who beware first dates are aware of this. How can we know if the other is authentic or merely sincere, charismatic or merely charming, when we know that both mock sincerity and faked charm are also everywhere? In fact, even the upfront disclosure of intent, performed artfully enough, can easily be used as yet one more tool in the armory of means to ends that discount the other. Ultimately, trust is always uncertain, even in a modest society, and something that takes time without the transparent indication, the heartwarming horizon, of an absolute surety. We can make a start at least, in

> ... that we recognize that our actions are always purposeful. And if a person wants to achieve a purpose, then he or she must also persuade others of it and, moreover, gain their consensus. Nevertheless, we have to be clear about whether we want to persuade others because we think it would be something good or whether we simply want to persuade them because it suits our purposes—without even asking whether this would be anything good. (Gadamer 2004:44)

In harnessing others to the action of one's own projects, we validate these latter's goodness, because the perspective of the other is brought into play as a leavening agent. Yet we can also enthrall others to such projects simply because they have the abilities to help these projects along instrumentally—their networks, their resources, their skills, or what have you. With the true Machiavellian intellect, it becomes difficult to tell these two intents apart. Only through repeated experience of usury can we understand the fact that we have been used, and perhaps for some, those humiliated in general and those humbled, we might never be able to grasp this essential difference. We are thus beholden to practice the modest avowal of projects that only *might* be good, and not those which we know up front are so, because this kind of absolute and a priori claim, while also not being modest, is also subject to abuse. On the one hand, if it proves not to be the case, with the enrollment of others and the enlistment of their abilities and resources, we let these others down and disappoint them in the cause they have taken up prematurely. And if the good be only in relation to the fact that we are actually using the rhetoric of goodness to promote a good only for the self, then we put the other in a position of being an object and acting contrary to their own goods. The sense that we might give over this dilemma to another realm remains strong even in modernity, because we also remain as weak in our ability to judge the good before it occurs to us as an event or an experience. Even then, we ourselves will change over time and what was once the good is good no longer. This is the nature of the ethical life, and it is pure chicanery to avoid the existential confrontation with it. In practicing the art of persuasion while remaining open to the other as both a course of resistance and critique reaffirms the value of all human life, not just one's own.

Our recent history has enlisted even the previous metaphysical figures in this cause: "This was intensified by the anthropocentric turn, where the purposes of God were narrowed to this one goal of sustaining human life. The continuing power of this idea if perhaps evident in the contemporary concern to preserve life, to bring prosperity, to reduce suffering, world-wide, which is I believe without precedent in world history." (Taylor 2007:370) The value of human life as an abstract concept allows us to sing paeans about it while doing relatively little to enhance specific persons' lives, especially if they are not are visible neighbors. We also have, in tandem with this reification of what in its most profound state is in fact something particular and real about the world as it is, the sense that what is of value need not be referential. That is, what is good is not necessarily measured by its effects in the world. This somewhat perverse stance becomes more understandable when we note that we have yet another thought in mind throughout this entire process of valuation, and that has to do with the more noble idea that, as Nietzsche suggests, "Greatness ought not to depend on success." (1983:113 [1874]) Rather, the way in which success is socially recognized is more likely to be a damper on our nobility, because we begin to follow the fame and fortune of those who praise us. In this, ironically, Nietzsche begins to sound very close to Augustine, and even uses a similar set of examples to further his point:

> The purest and truest adherents of Christianity have always hindered and called into question its worldly success and so-called "power in history" rather than promoted them; for they were accustomed to place themselves outside the "world" and had no regard for the "process of the Christian idea"; for which reason they have as a rule remained wholly unknown and anonymous to history. (ibid:114)

It is likely that each of us knows, or perhaps even is oneself, a person whose good works go unacknowledged. When they do come to light, sometimes long after the death of the person in question, we are reminded of how much work goes on in human relations "behind the scenes," as it were. This noble effort may even give the impression that when elites go behind the scenes to work some magic in their favor, we are more comfortable with this than perhaps we should be, because we imagine that the good or the noble is being enacted simply due to its apparently anonymous quality. The good might even be tainted, or yet perverted, if we should have to not only persuade the other of its inherent value but also convince the other that our intents toward the good are without ulterior motive. In the case of elites of any sector, we are aware that such motives are in fact present. Yet even here these usually self-seeking motives become more noble by the fact that they do not have to hide themselves once already behind closed doors. This being private to be public is mimicked by the rest of us in contexts such as the Internet, the bedroom, or the club. Here we can be sincere, or, if we wish to be insincere, we need not hide that from others either. We can, if you will, be sincere in our insincerity. Akin to being secure in our insecurity, or open about our intolerance, honest about our dishonesty, the making noble of values by leaving them unacknowledged in various ways is a manner of play-acting modesty. It is duplicitous due to fact that we actually desire, like the aforementioned pessimist, to see an outcome that we publicly deny. We perhaps wish for the good to be noticed and to even be rewarded, but understand the good as being more authentic if it remains in an occlusive pariah status.

In order to justify ignoring the works of good people we also maintain the sense that having a virtue is its own recompense. Lately, being "virtual" is also its own reward, given the ability to role-play one's way through this other reality, this second life. The sense that a persona connotes what reality there is for us in the social world has been well developed by sociologists. Yet for regular people, there is often a sense that one does ultimately "come home to oneself from being otherwise." Indeed, we are touched and moved by the appearance of sincerity and modesty, whatever may consist the substantive material at hand: "But the popular emphasis on sincerity means more than this. It means that the source of criteria for judgement has shifted from the content of the performance and its goodness or badness, aesthetically speaking, to the personality of the performer. He is judged for his attitude toward the audience, an attitude which is either sincere or insincere." (Riesman 1950:220)

The "good" person then becomes the person who is good at looking good, or less tritely, we become part of the good in itself by making what has been good about ourselves part of "making good" in the world, that is, part of being successful. To have "made it good" still means success, materially or systemically, with regard to social status and social esteem, as well as access to the various forms of capital in modernity. To "make *the* good," means rather, to enact goodness in the world. Although we might take this as a little old-fashioned—and perhaps this is yet another reason why we are happy to hide it away for the purposes of posterity or for its own unknowable tomb—we do still remark upon the difference between greatness and success, just as Nietzsche and Augustine, amongst others, have done before us. This also allows us to become authentically modest, rather than humble or humiliated by enacting our relative merit on a broader than normative spectrum. Just as when we feel oppressed or downtrodden, we can gain perspective and perhaps even courage by knowing the stories of others who may live in contexts that we would regard as unlivable; by contrasting our lot and our abilities with those who have much more and much less than we, we realize the modesty of the general human condition, and ourselves as the local vehicle for it. I am reminded of the end of Neil Peart's acceptance speech at the 1994 Juno Awards for being given the lifetime achievement award as a member of the popular band Rush. It went something like this: "Nietzsche once said that without music, life would be a mistake. I can add that without music, I would have to get a life, and without our fans, I would have to get a job." Indeed, we are dimly aware that whatever our respective talents, we are more or less wholly reliant on others to either affirm or reject them, with often serious consequences either way. This is modesty once again appearing as a mode of being human. It is realistic in its appraisal of the situation, and comes to us directly from the world as it is, and not indirectly from the one which we desire to be, or in the service of the one we would force upon others. No matter the scale of fame and fortune—though those at the higher ends of these scales are more able to forget their relations to others—each of our accomplishments is a work of many authors.

This is perhaps one of the major reasons why we cannot ever say to ourselves that we have completely done something on our own, for better or worse. The responsibility may lie with us, to be sure, and perhaps we are best capable of being responsible for this or that action or event, once again, for better or for worse, but no human project is a singularity, unless death itself can be termed part of the human project. Along with the sense that every human being has experience and ability of some kind, and hence a knowledge of some sort about something, the idea that we are participating in a collective, though conflicting, effort resounds all the more boldly when we ourselves are modest about our parts in the whole. Even those to whom are granted the status of knowledge, or the ability to know, are very much part of this process, and may not even be the most conscious of it:

> I always feel uncomfortable when people expect the philosopher to be presumptuous enough to claim to know what nobody else recognizes or understands, or even to know better than anyone else what first needs to be done. In my opinion philosophical thinking simply consists in making what we all already know another step more conscious. But this means, too, that philosophers do not know everything and this recognition itself leaves us that much less likely to be tempted to misuse the knowledge and skills we presume ourselves to possess. (Gadamer 1996:139)

The rest of us who are not charged historically as being the fonts of wisdom or social critique may, obviously, think the same of ourselves regarding our abilities. This is modesty without humility. It is simply realistic to note, and to continue to be aware, that none of us has all of the necessary knowledge to perform every task with which we are confronted, or to have experienced all possible outcomes of such actions. If each of us is an amateur social philosopher in this way, with partial knowledge striving to become more impartial, then the very process of how we come to understand our situation with regard to others makes us ever the student of living on. No other kind of knowledge is quite like this, as each of these others, the sciences in particular, involve also a specific set of techniques for discovering the truths about the world, cosmos, and our place in it. These kinds of skills must be formally learned not merely as techniques, to be sure, but as well as worldviews and attitudes and even types of ethical reflections. They are not held within us due only to our heritage of being human and growing into a common humanity:

> Clearly it belongs to the essence of philosophy in contrast to the other sciences that it raises questions which we cannot eliminate even if we do not know how to answer them. In this sense the question concerning the nature pf philosophy is itself a philosophical question to which we have no answer. Whatever philosophy is, it must be seen as a natural propensity within us all rather than as some sort of professional skill or ability. (ibid:93)

The methods of other forms of knowing and the statements of other forms of discourse all seek in part to explain and answer specific questions. That they do so remarkably well in spite of the limitations of their own paradigms, the limits of our current technological prostheses, and the limiting factor of our own finite lifetimes, sometimes makes us think that all questions can be definitively responded to by human beings and their sciences. Yet this is likely to prove immodest, and would be merely the obverse of some more traditional manner of knowing that seeks not to question in the face of the humility of our apparent cosmic insignificance. So we must rather try to avoid reacting to the once only humble beginnings of human knowledge with the overcompensation that woos us with the sense that what is now human knowledge can in fact be all and know all.

Along with the scientific quest for truth, there has been the recent attempt on an increasingly massive scale to improve the quality of human life by removing injustice and physical deprivation from the world. Sometimes these two threads of our now modern consciousness are imbricated in one another, as when we look to medical science or engineering technology to cure us from this illness or save us from that onerous labor. By trial and error, we gradually learned a new kind of belief. This is not only a belief in ourselves, or a belief that by improving our lot we are doing God's assigned work on earth, but a belief that we can know has real effects. Of course, we have the voices of millions to fall back on here, just as we know there are suppressed voices of perhaps still many more that are not as of yet benefiting from this new attitude we have taken up regarding our merits. Not only this, but ". . . what also ran parallel, and which perhaps doesn't astonish us enough, was the belief that all this could be accomplished. How was it, in the face of so much violence and disorder, both in history and in the present, in the face of such obvious refractory human material, that people could entertain serious hopes of making a decisive, even irreversible change for the better?" (Taylor 2007:119)

Needless to say, such changes which have been wrought in both the arenas of scientific knowledge and general human consequences of the use of such knowledge have been hardly without reverse. Regressions of the most grotesque sort have occurred, and the shadow of ultimate nuclear apocalypse harbors the fact that others as yet unimagined are still possible for us to enact. Yet we cannot be tempted to see these as inhuman blights upon the lighted course of what is truly human. They are part of us, and not part of any particular historical guise of ourselves. This is why they are still present today. They may be called authentically "historical" because indeed, they do not seem to have been extant in any serious way before the invention of agriculture and the development of large-scale agrarian irrigation civilizations, which was also hallmarked by the birth of the written word. They may have occurred on a much smaller scale—intertribal warfare, slavery, and caste-like kinship are all well-known ethnographic facts hailing from some pre-agrarian societies around the world—but what is of essence for our mindset today is the division between light and dark, good and evil.

The idea then that what is painful for us, or what produces suffering both for ourselves and others, is inherently a bad thing, a wrong action, is an idea that seems to have its genesis in the metaphysics of agrarianism, where the first large-scale religious institutions appear, and the first ideas of gods as aloof to and beyond human affairs come into being. In a word, we believe that we can do good or its opposite, simply by acting within the usual human ambit of what we know as action. More than this—and this is the most profound meaning of the origin myths that cast humans as fallen because of the encounter with the nature of human knowledge and thus its mortal limits and values—we understand our knowledge to be the knowledge of the good and the bad, and not merely "knowledge itself," as if this body of discourse is given life only through application. "Knowledge for its own sake" is, of course, still a noble venture, but the "sake" in this proverbial phrase includes the human value spectrum of ethics. In other words, the value of knowing is built into not only the ability to know but also what comes of this ability. This is the true "itself" of knowledge: "Does not the highest human value consist in recognizing one's own limits and being open to what is unforeseeable? Paying respect to human modesty in contrast to the modern claim of measureless omnipotence . . ." (Grondin 2003:286)

In doing so, we not only range our affairs against a set of techniques that proclaim unlimited mastery, but we also have to step back from similar claims once accorded more fully to the nonhuman realm of the gods. Whatever resonance of this period in human history, just summarized, is now seen in the light of doubt precisely because of the advent of the scientific method and the methods of philosophical rationalism and empiricism. More than this, there is the increased encounter with the often bitter experience of being human itself. When "nice guys finish last" in any serious manner, we are left to question the validity of statements concerning ultimate justice, even though we are suspicious that this is in fact why we invented those notions for ourselves in the first place. Yet we cannot abandon such ideas as whole cloth, simply because it was those *same* ideas—in their aspiration toward the imagined perfection of the divinity—that led us forward to the inventions of science and social justice:

> For those who cannot accept the Christian hope of a reconciliation beyond history, and who cannot any more believe in the various formulae of double harmony in our earthly condition, the conclusion might seem clear: abandon all hopes of such harmony. But this leaves a lot indeterminate. What more modest hopes are left? And can one really bring oneself to abandon these goals? Does not a great deal of our political activity take as its goal, if only as an idea of reason, a world order in which peoples live together in quality and justice? Does not a great deal of our efforts at healing take as a goal the wholeness of the person? How easily can we set these goals aside? (Taylor 2007:617)

There is a difference between a hope and a goal, of course. The one can remain vague, even ethereal if need be to foster its continued relevance to the nitty gritty of human affairs. But the other one is the outcome of a plan, the end of a series of means, and therefore becomes more real the more we think about its realization. There is an inertia at work here, a kind of positive self-fulfilling prophecy, in that when we believe we can accomplish something we tend to be surprised and disappointed if in fact we cannot. *All the more reason to accomplish the task,* we tell ourselves; there is also a healthy amount of egotism involved perhaps even in the most noble works of humanity, including those that are directed at the well-being of others. It is all very well to pretend to an ethics that negates the self-interested aspect of us in the act, but it is not always necessary to do so. If self-negation is the highest of goods in this sphere, then let it be so just for the moment it takes to give oneself over to the other. Otherwise there is the risk of humility and humiliation, the intrusive coercion of the other in myself, and thence my corresponding lack of ability to return home to myself through the other. Returning home is not a flight from otherness to what we knew as ourselves, but rather must be a journey in which we take the other back to what we now are. We show this aspect of otherness what we have become. Needless to say, encounters with the other often provoke a flight, especially when we are faced with that which threatens our comfortable equanimity. The confrontation with the other in the present is the same, as we have said above, as the confrontation with tradition in history. We must be willing to risk ourselves with the knowledge that we will temporarily lose ourselves. Given the world situation, this is our utmost challenge:

> The negative, self-defensive response to this is to shut a lot of it out; don't watch the evening news for a while, concentrate on something else. More corrosively,

> throughout history we have been good at cancelling the horror by telling ourselves that these people are not really like us; maybe they don't really mind the poverty and squalor as we would; or maybe they're bad, they're evil, and they deserve it; or they brought it on themselves through their sloth and fecklessness. Or else we paint a brighter picture of things, in which the suffering is occluded; for instance, we distance ourselves through an external, aestheticizing vision of the natives in their meaningful, thick culture. (ibid:681)

A consistent alertness to the human condition in all of its manifold suffering is likely to wear one out, even to the point of cynicism. In the same way, however, we begin to become shallow when we are attentive only to the joys of life. Neither the dark glass nor the light one alone is ultimately fulfilling for us, because even if we affirm only the shadows of the human spirit or completely negate them with the "brighter picture" of fantasy and romance, we remain aware at some level the contrived quality of our living on. We know there is more to life than what we desire to see, because the very presence of desire in us pushes us onward to something that is not yet present. We desire because we do not possess, and what we do not possess at the moment is the clue that the world is more than what it appears to be for us. Perhaps the most famous incarnation of the manner in which desire acts as leverage for both a fuller human being and a fuller reality is the idea of a community "beyond itself," as it were. The archetypical parable of the enactment of such a community is of course the "good" Samaritan, although one raises one's eyebrows a little at the implication that the average Samaritan is, if not bad, at least not usually good either: "… what has always been stressed in Christian agape is that it can take us beyond the bounds of any already existing solidarity. The Good Samaritan was in no way bound to the man he helped. That was, indeed, the point of the story." (ibid:246) That is, he was not bound by social conventions or even by the alternative ethics of his time, and for that matter, our own. Yet, in reaching out, he transgresses social boundaries and creates a new ethics. The metaphysical implication here is, of course, that in failing to recognize social boundaries, we cast them as "merely human," constructed by ourselves for ourselves. In order to "get beyond" these we need to take up an ethics that has a supra-human origin—that is, one designed by a god or the gods. Yet we know that this idea does not necessarily follow from transgression, as human history is replete with examples of rule breakers of the most diverse kind. To hitch our transgressions up to a prime mover is to negate the ethics of the Samaritan. "Go and do likewise" is manifestly a social injunction, however revolutionary and charismatic, and it might not even be in fact ethical to also see it as one divine.

The ability to change society and social relations is built into the notion of transgression. It also is a function of desire. We do not yet have the kind of society we wish to have. We must break the current rules of our social organization, or at least some of the most onerous of them, in order to get what we want. "Can we get there from here?" is a question that we constantly ask of ourselves, both as a culture and within our individuated biographies. That we are not at all certain of being able to respond in the affirmative is part of the character of both desire and transgression. Indeed, the thrill of the chase is in not knowing how it will turn out, as much as the result already takes shape in our imaginations, especially if we have had prior kindred experiences. The fact that we desire something of another, whether that otherness is a human being, an institution, a society, or a god, always comes home to the sense that we desire a change in ourselves. We wish to become other than what we currently are, and it is in this desire that we come home to ourselves through all of the others just listed. Each approach to an other thus involves a transgression of the boundaries we have erected about ourselves, as well as those that have been in place surrounding us as social reality and historical tradition. Of course, it is not enough merely to have this desire. One must also be aware of the fact that the other does not exist to fulfill oneself, that what is not already of myself cannot be hijacked or kidnapped with the express and sole purpose of helping me attain the other being that I imagine myself willing to become. Instead,

> ... the genuine meaning of our finitude or our "thrownness" consists in the fact that we become aware, not only of our being historically conditioned, but especially of our being conditioned by the other. Precisely in our ethical relation to the other, it becomes clear to us how difficult it is to do justice to the demands of the other or even simply to become aware of them. The only way not to succumb to our finitude is to open ourselves to the other, to listen to the "thou" who stands before us. (Gadamer 2004:29)

Within the reach of what is human lies the paradoxical amalgam of what we know to be kindred to ourselves and what also appears to be unlike anything we have known. We are given perspective by the additional presence of the truly nonhuman otherness of nature and cosmos, and the alternative being of what we imagine to be the more than human otherness of potential inhabitants of this nature and perhaps of natures we are yet to understand. The wider cosmos demands of us an ethics that recognizes our modest place within it, while local nature reminds us that modesty is necessary for the survival of our shared ecosystems. Finally, the presence of the human other places us already and always into an ethics that alerts us to that which we lack, and to that which can only be understood as human in the humaneness of genuine dialogue and community, unconstrained by parochial social boundaries.

In light of these perspectives, I am reminded of a brief experience I had many years ago in the Mississippi Delta. I was a member of a poker group which had been founded some thirty years before I encountered it. Indeed, some of its founding members were dead by the time I participated in its good-natured stereotypically masculine "burlesque." Games went well into the early hours, and as I drove home across the alluvial plain I would be privy to the nocturnal meanderings of animals and stars alike. I once deliberately drove to a point on this route at the farthest margin between villages, so no man-made light could impinge on the view. I shut off the car and stepped outside to gaze in awe at the Milky Way and its attendant arms and nebulae, their beauty seemingly beyond human judgment and ken. The vastness of even our tiny local niche in the universe could very well be seen as overwhelming, but I was made aware of another nature, much closer to my side. The night was also the time of most of the other creatures with which we share this home. It was their otherness which produced anxiety, and not the distant and aloof, and entirely nonthreatening, canopy of firmament. Would a panther suddenly leap out of the groves, or a crocodile, wild boar, or, more benignly, a startling bat? Perhaps I should die here on the spot, while contemplating a cosmos that itself stretches beyond any known finitude. A faint prickling under my skin drove me back into my vehicle, my at first calculated and then wondrous experience truncated. Anxiety in the face of the other is not an end in itself, but rather the means to begin again the journey toward a horizon that is ever afar though it ever beckons. Gadamer (1996:162) reminds us that "The life which awakens to thinking and questioning thinks and questions beyond all limits. To know anxiety and to be made to grasp death, this is the human birth cry which never wholly dies away."

Epilogue: The Post-Nuclear Age

BACK IN 1983, ABC and Hollywood co-produced the television film *The Day After*, which documented the run up to, and the aftermath of, a cold war–inspired nuclear holocaust. The result was disconcertingly effective, and the airing of this feature actually had real effects in the realm of the popular political culture of the time. The film ends with a little note on screen that contains both a hope and a caveat, in that the producers felt that it should be taken as inspiring another path to avoid such events, but that also a real nuclear war would in fact be even worse in its devastation than what was so graphically portrayed in the film. Due to many other more powerful factors, within two years of its release, the final heat of the cold war had dissipated, glasnost and perestroika had seen their advent, and the general world economy had turned around for the time being. Watching the film again after a full quarter-century I was struck much more violently and emotionally than I had been at age seventeen, in my final year of high school. I recalled that most of the schools in North America shut down their regular classes for "the day after *The Day After*," as it was billed, to attempt to reassure children that what they had seen was unlikely because adults knew that the consequences were so terrible and terrifying. Smuggled into these sessions, at least in some schools, there were critiques of the geopolitics of the day and a call to protest the unearthly fate that humans had proclaimed for themselves as one of the major outcomes of the previous world war.

Yet we at that age had already grown fatalistic about such events; we might even have been said to have expected them in some form or other. The evidence of this attitude was everywhere. When I matriculated to the local university the next year, for example, the student union had stockpiled cyanide pills in its building on campus for distribution in case of crisis. This service was withdrawn after my first two years as an undergraduate, given the changing world situation. The student body was imagined to be receptive to the idea of mass suicide, which, given the knowledge of the likely results of a nuclear exchange, was probably realistic. We had no real need for pills in Victoria, Canada, though, as the city was the home to the nation's Pacific Fleet naval base and sundry other military sites. Only Canada, yes, but no doubt a head on target for one of the thousands of Soviet warheads that both cold war sides had made sure they had enough of to leave quite literally no stone unturned. Indeed, we were as safe as anyone could be, with the reality of certain and instantaneous death hanging over our heads. We knew that near its epicenter even a small nuclear weapon explosion would vaporize organic life. A bit farther afield, one would be flash-burned to blackened ash in the outline of one's skeleton. Yet further away one could expect to be incinerated in a few moments, further still knocked unconscious and burned to death, then killed by the shock wave and charred by the heat, then blinded, deafened, and rendered unconscious by the blast, as one moved farther away from the site of the burst. With any of these, death would be more or less instantaneous, without pain or suffering. It was those who survived the attack who would be the truest victims, as they would die in an agonizing evolution of radiation burns and poisoning, blindness and emotional alienation, knowing that loved ones and the world alike were gone forever. One does not really "survive" nuclear war.

We have constructed this situation for ourselves due mainly to the belief in linear history and the telescoped understanding of our mytho-poetic narratives in the West. We are aware of our origins as fallen, and we anticipate our ends as judged. The ability to contrive the apocalypse is based on our belief that the end of the species is an apocalyptic one. We have come perilously close to fulfilling our myths, while in fact denying the entire history of our species, that history which, in its most humane fullness, shows us to be amazingly skilled, curious, intrepid, and courageous folk, with enormous capability for compassion and the reflective overcoming of our once animal instincts. When we became aware of the scientific depth of our presence on the earth, and when we were able to look at the earth from afar, as a whole image, for the first time, we began to realize that petty divisions and the competition over resources promoted by the institutions of our latter-day tribal nations were in fact beneath us, as characters who would rather live on and perhaps live as one. The first human communities needed all of the nascent appurtenances of culture to survive. Each simple technology was a boon to human life. Our situation is both the same and different. We need our knowledge every bit as desperately as our ancient ancestors needed theirs, but today our knowledge must include the limits of knowledge, and the limits of human capabilities of destruction which currently have, with regard to our collective mortality, no limits.

In choosing to vindicate and support certain concepts over others, we set in motion historical forces of which we have, at best, a translucent understanding. Better to choose those ideas that we know today, no matter their oft perverse and manipulated extremities and manifestations, to be more sound and more reflective of both our ability to think and of the world as it is. We face the reality of conflict each day, but the modest society would limit the means to engage in aggression: To the thought of anti-ballistic missiles and fighter-interceptors, anti-armor missiles and helicopters, anti-missile destroyers such as the Royal Navy's new Type 45, and defensive frigates, a qualified *yes*, but to Intercontinental Ballistic Missiles (ICBM), fighter-bombers and strategic bombers, main battle armor and attack helicopters, aircraft carriers and nuclear submarines, an unqualified *no*. To be rational, ethical, brave, skeptical, prudent, to engage in critique, and to be modest is to take the stance that humanity is at its best when the humane understanding of oneself as another is paramount. Through this, we distinguish ourselves from all that we could also be and all that we know we are still. The shadowy propensities of the human condition cannot be denied, but they need not be exacerbated. The suffering of both the one and the many cannot be suppressed, but it need not be calculated. The ultimate mortality of all human life cannot be overcome, but it need not be personified as a determined design. No doubt we, each of us, resent at least a little the fact that we must die. We would like to live on, even for a little while longer. But it is a *ressentiment* against human life itself, which includes the consciousness of its own demise, to render this personal anxiety and resentment in a manner larger than life. Others have the right to live on even when we find that we cannot accompany them further. They will take our species where we could not, but they too know that they tread farther because we aided their earlier journeys, and that they too will pass the vision to those who follow, and to those who they in turn have aided.

In doing so, we are slowly entering the "post-nuclear" age. In 1960, the United States census reported that only 60 percent of Americans lived in nuclear families and this at the height of the *Leave It to Beaver* popular culture. In 2000, the census states that only 24 percent are in the same kind of family, and the trend is continuing to drop off. As well, in the interim, we have mapped and begun to understand the subatomic, quantum reality of that which makes up nuclear particles. We have returned to family forms that dominated periods before capitalism, though we have invented new variations on them, and we have also stepped forward into the uncannily flavored world of the quark and the boson. As this book goes to press, the United States and Russia have agreed to hold new talks on reducing strategic arms. They are too expensive to maintain, for one. Could it be that, in part due to the acquisitive character of capitalist elites, the hoarding of wealth and the lack of taxation, such could have this wonderfully positive, though latent, effect? It would be perhaps ironic that the same kind of abilities and justifications that were important in propelling the potential apocalypse also were important in dismantling its threat. Yet we should not be so surprised; for the entirety of human history of which we are aware, our dual natures have come to the fore to both endanger us and to remove us from harm. The question of "human nature" today is more immanent than ever before, due to the momentary character of the forces within which we negotiate our continuing presence. We avoid failure by increasingly thin margins of error, and the tools at our disposal for life and for death are immediately available should we choose mistakenly, without regard for the consequences of our failure.

  We ultimately would fail ourselves, for these are not the tools of the hand of a God who would destroy us for having failed Him, but are merely the tools of the hand of Man who would destroy himself for imagining that he had failed.

Cited and Suggested Reading

Arendt, Hannah. *Men in Dark Times.* New York: Harcourt, Brace, and Jovanovich, 1968.

Atwood, Margaret. *Payback: Debt and the Shadow Side of Wealth.* Toronto: Harper Collins (House of Anansi Press), 2008.

Berger, Peter. *Invitation to Sociology: An Humanistic Perspective.* New York: Anchor Books, 1963.

Dawkins, Richard. *The God Delusion.* New York: Houghton Mifflin, 2006.

Durkheim, Emile. *On Morality and Society.* Robert Bellah, ed. Chicago: The University of Chicago Press, 1973 [1914].

Gadamer, Hans-Georg. *A Century of Philosophy: a conversation with Riccardo Dottori.* New York: Continuum Books, 2004 [2000].

_____. *Gadamer in Conversation: Reflections and Commentary.* Richard E. Palmer, ed. New Haven, Conn.: Yale University Press, 2001 [1999].

_____. "The Ethics of Value and Practical Philosophy," in *Hermeneutics, Religion, and Ethics.* New Haven, Conn.: Yale University Press, 1999 [1982]: 103–18.

_____. *The Enigma of Health: The Art of Healing in a Scientific Age*. Stanford, Calif.: Stanford University Press, 1996 [1993].

Grondin, Jean. *Hans-Georg Gadamer: A Biography*. New Haven, Conn.: Yale University Press, 2003.

Loewen, G. V. *What Is God? Musings on Human Anxiety and Aspiration*. New York: AEG Strategic Book Publishers, 2008.

_____. "Belief in Desireful Violence as Means of Self-Discipline and Empowerment," in *How Can We Explain the Persistence of Irrational Beliefs? Essays in Social Anthropology*. Lewiston, N.Y.: The Edwin Mellen Press, 2006: 137–68.

Mills, C. Wright. *White Collar*. Oxford: Oxford University Press (Galaxy Books), 1956.

Nietzsche, Friedrich. *On the Future of our Educational Institutions*. South Bend, Ind.: St. Martin's Press, 2004 [1872].

_____. "On the Uses and Disadvantages of History for Life," in *Untimely Meditations*. R.J. Hollingdale, ed.. Cambridge: Cambridge University Press, 1968 [1874]: 57–124.

Riesman, David. *The Lonely Crowd: A Study of the Changing American Character*. New Haven, Conn.: Yale University Press, 1950.

Ritzer, George. *The McDonaldization of Society*. New York: Pine Forge Press, 1996.s

Sagan, Carl. *The Demon-Haunted World: Science as a Candle in the Dark*. New York: Ballantine Books, 1996.

Scheler, Max. *Ressentiment*. Marquette University Press, Milwaukee, Wisconsin, 2003 [1912].

Stein, Janet Gross. *The Cult of Efficiency*. Toronto: Harper Collins (House of Anansi Press), 2001.

Taylor, Charles. *A Secular Age.* Cambridge, Mass.: Harvard University Press (Belknap Press), 2007.

Weber, Max. "Science as a Vocation," in *From Max Weber: Essays in Sociology,* 2nd edition. Hans Gerth and C. Wright Mills, eds. Oxford: University Press (Galaxy Books), 1958 [1919]: 129–56.